Adventures

of an

Alaskan Preacher

WAYNE COGGINS

 MAGNUS PRESS

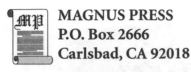 **MAGNUS PRESS**
P.O. Box 2666
Carlsbad, CA 92018

www.magnuspress.com

Adventures of an Alaskan Preacher

First Edition, 2007

Printed in the United States of America

Scripture quotations taken from The Amplified New Testament ®, Copyright ©1958 by The Lockman Foundation. Used by permission. (www.Lockman.org)

Scripture quotations taken from the HOLY BIBLE, NEW INTERNATIONAL VERSION, Copyright © 1973, 1978, 1984 by International Bible Society. Used by permission of the International Bible Society.

LCCN: 2006940579
ISBN: 978-0-9724869-5-8

Publisher's Cataloging-In-Publication Data
(Prepared by The Donohue Group, Inc.)

Coggins, Wayne.
  Adventures of an Alaskan preacher / by Wayne Coggins. — 1st ed.

  p. ; cm.

  ISBN: 978-0-9724869-5-8

  1. Clergy—Alaska—Anecdotes. 2. Christian life—Anecdotes.
3. Trust in God. 4. Spiritual life. I. Title.

BV4517 .C64 2007
248.4
2006940579

---

11 10 09 08 07   10 9 8 7 6 5 4 3 2

To my wonderful wife

❧ *Marveen* ☙

who is truly a gift from God

TABLE OF CONTENTS

ACKNOWLEDGMENTS

God doesn't waste anything, including the work and creativity He puts into setting up learning experiences for His children. In my lifetime, I have, in retrospect, seen the hand of God at work by taking what seemed like random events and difficult times and funnel them down into a few moments when those lessons learned are just the ticket to help a fellow journeyperson through their own difficulties.

Thank Yous and Acknowledgments

I want to express my gratitude for the people that God has put in my life along the way that have been willing to walk with me for awhile and share their own lives and experiences so that I might benefit. I want to thank my former wife, Barbara Christy, who for 21 years bravely ventured with me into adulthood, Alaska and beyond. Though no longer my wife, she is the mother of our three children and as such, I honor her. I want to thank my current wife, Marveen, who has spent the last 15 years with me, living our dreams, and teaching me what it means to slow down and enjoy the journey. It is her love, sacrifice, and encouragement that enabled me to finish my college degrees and keep plodding along with this writing project. Her heart is big enough to embrace her stepchildren and their families as though they were her own. What a treasure she is.

Tracie, Michele and David, are three incredibly gifted kids, each in their own unique way. I am immensely proud to be their dad. Their children, our grandchildren, are special beyond words.

My mom, Eileen, has lived the life and walked the talk of genuine Christianity for all of her life and mine. She is love personified and shared it freely with my dad for fifty years. My dad, Glenn Coggins, was one of the wisest and perhaps the kindest man I have ever known. He is with the Lord now, but not before he modeled for us kids what dads are supposed to be like. I have been blessed to have my brother, Mark, and sisters, Glenice and Judy, all of whom serve the Lord and love their families with all of their hearts . . . and still find time to encourage me on a regular basis.

I have had perhaps more than an average allotment of terrific friends over the years who have stuck with me through thick and thin. I can't mention them all, but I must say that Gene Evans, before he took an early exit to heaven, proved to be the best and most loyal friend a person could have.

I also want to again thank my wife, Marveen, who, along with my good friends, Sally McMahan Pollen and Dr. Eva Evans, have encouraged me to keep writing even though they could spot my double negatives and dangling participles from fifty paces. I also appreciate greatly the nudges to write from Doris McMillon, Steve Rinehart, Mary Pat Murphy, Jim Morrison, Rick Kardos and my good friends and fellow pastors, Brian Chronister, Terry Hill, Hilmer Kiser, Rob Ryg, Rick and Dick Benjamin, Richard Irwin, Sid Glasscock and the pastor's group I meet with weekly in Nikiski. As a young man, when looking for a role model as a pastor, Warren Carlsen was the man. A man's man and a man of God. . . Thank you, Warren, for your lifetime of courageous Christian ministry. "May heaven's best be your daily portion" was your trademark greeting. May it return to you a hundredfold.

I offer my thanks also to the many people who allowed me to tell their story as it intertwined with mine. It is to the friends and supporters of Cornerstone Family Ministries that I express my heartfelt thanks for your support over the past twenty years, and specifically for the finances to get this book project underway. Thank you to the folks at Magnus Press for stepping out with me on this. Without them, most of these stories would likely have faded and been lost when I died. Most important of all, I thank God, for His incredible mercy and grace and His love that hasn't given up on me.

Finally, I need to add that all of the stories in this book are true. A few names, places and other identifying factors have been altered to protect the innocent or the guilty. If you are reading this book, *you* are an answer to my prayers.

PREFACE

"Alaska! Who would ever want to go to that god-forsaken, frozen iceberg of a place to live?" I think that was my first thought when an old college friend asked me if I were interested in coming to Alaska with him. He was just passing through the Seattle area and decided to see if I was interested in some adventure. What he knew little of, was that at 25 years old my life had been spiraling downward into some miserable circumstances. I had just prayed, "Lord, if you will show me the exit ramp out of this place, I'll take it!" Like a flashbulb going off in my head, I knew this *exit ramp* said, "Alaska—Turn Here."

A week later I was on my way with him up the Alaska Highway, and we arrived in Anchorage on Thanksgiving Day, 1971. I remember a sign on a shopping mall reader board that displayed the temperature as 24 degrees! What had I gotten myself into?

Within a few days I had a job working the graveyard shift at a local gas station and freezing my fingers and toes off. For recreation, I would park at the end of the runway at the airport and watch planes take off while wishing I was on one taking me someplace, anyplace warm!

Within a few months my wife and daughters arrived and I found myself the newly selected rookie pastor of a little church at the "end of the road" in Homer, Alaska. The adventure had begun that would take me to just about every corner of this huge land on assignments that I believe originated with God. From the southeastern cities of Juneau and Sitka to the northernmost reaches of Prudhoe Bay, far north of the Arctic Circle, I kept saying "yes" to invitations to minister. From the far western village of Nome to the interior town of Fairbanks, more opportunities came. From the big city of Anchorage to the small towns of Homer, Seward and Nikiski on the Kenai Peninsula, wide open doors presented themselves. A lifetime later, I don't feel very old, but I think I certainly am a high-mileage model!

In my wildest imagination, I don't think I could have dreamed up the twists and turns of life that Alaska had to offer. Raised on a little farm in western Washington, I had never been on an airplane, nor did I know there was more than one way to cook a steak. Little did I know that my future would include walking away from a plane crash, looking down the barrel of a loaded gun and sampling raw whale blubber! Wildlife to me was an occasional deer or skunk in the chicken coop—not Alaskan grizzlies stalking me or a moose in my backyard. Raised near a steelhead and salmon stream in the Northwest, I would have thought it impossible to catch a limit of six salmon in a half-hour or bring home a 70-1/2 lb. king salmon.

I am too young to start thinking in terms of "memoirs" or my life story being preserved as some sort of legacy. I have faith that the best is yet to come and the adventure has just begun. What I present to you in this book is sort of a mid-stream glimpse of how the journey has gone so far. These are true stories of my adventures as a pastor in the far flung reaches of the Alaskan wilderness. You'll enjoy meeting some of the colorful characters that have given Alaska its nickname as . . . The Greatland!

CHAPTER 1

In the Crosshairs

In my thirty-five years of pastoring in the far north, one thing I can say for sure is that it has been anything but boring! Oh, there have been those moments of feeling isolated and frustrated by the long hours of winter darkness, but there has never been a lack of action or adventure. When I read Paul's account in 2 Corinthians 11:26 about being in "perils" of various kinds, I can relate.

In the Crosshairs . . . Nome, AK

Back in the early seventies I had an exciting assignment as an interim pastor in Nome, a predominately Inupiat Eskimo village on the Bering Sea not all that far from Siberia. It was a very interesting experience to say the least—learning about the local customs and culture including sampling some of the local food that is a bit of a challenge if you are not used to it. Muk-tuk (whale), Oogrook (bearded seal) and Eskimo doughnuts (cooked in seal oil) were all on the menu of our "welcome to Nome" reception. I was keenly aware that all eyes were watching to see if I were willing to give their type of food a try. It actually wasn't bad but I had to enlist a can of Pepsi to help get the muk-tuk past my Adam's apple!

A few months into my time there I had decided to go ptarmigan (a small bird, white in winter, that is similar to grouse) hunting along the road a few miles out of town. I had seen large flocks of them in the willow bushes out that direction numerous times. As I was driving along I noticed a small flock of birds take off and soar around the back side of a small hill, so I parked and set out afoot on the hard crusted snow to see if I could bag dinner. When I got to where the birds had landed, they saw me first and flew out of sight.

As I was trudging back toward my vehicle, I noticed that a pick-up truck had parked next to me and there was a man standing alongside it eyeing me with binoculars. As I approached him I swallowed hard when I saw that he now had a rifle in his hands and it was pointed directly at me. I had no idea what possessed him to want to point that thing my direction, but I soon discovered why.

Without lowering the rifle (by the size of the bore, I guessed it was a 30.06 caliber), he asked me in broken English who I was and what (expletive) I was doing hunting in his territory?! By his speech and manner, I could tell that my situation was precarious at best.

Have you ever been in one of those positions when you are in need of some instant assistance from the Lord and you discover you can pray a hundred miles an hour and never move your lips? This was one of those times.

It turned out that this man was a reindeer herder and they had been having some problems with rustlers. (I know this may sound like an old cowboy movie plot, but it is the truth.) He was assuming that no one in their right mind would be out hunting birds in that country, so I must be a rustler.

I frantically tried to explain to him who I was and what I was doing which was a bit of a struggle with a loaded rifle pointed at my chest. Beyond a doubt the Lord intervened as I began to explain to him how I was friends with several of the village's most respected elders who were members of my church, all of whom were known by him.

After a few (eternally long to me) seconds, he slowly lowered the muzzle of his weapon, grinned, and gave me some wise advice that I should check with him if I were ever going to hunt birds around that area again. I was all nods and smiles and gratitude as I got in the car, turned around and headed back to town. I was not negligent to express profuse thanks to God for helping me out of that one. When I got back home and started to get out of the truck, my knees and legs felt like Jell-O from the aftermath of a major adrenaline jolt!!

It was years later that I learned a very interesting bit of information that the Lord had used to bail me out of that situation. If you ask most people who live in the western culture of America who they are, you will likely hear their name and what they do for a living. We are often defined by our jobs. In the Inupiat Eskimo culture, who you are is defined more by who your father, uncles, grandparents or friends are than by what you do for a living. It is a sign of respect to inquire after the well-being of those individuals. What I had done (unbeknownst to me but not to God) was to invoke the names of men who were highly respected in that area, and in so doing I had won a reprieve for myself.

There is awesome power available to us in the name of Jesus. And, it doesn't hurt if you are ever in Western Alaska to know the names of Joshua Awinona, Dwight Milligrok, Tommy Ongtooguk and Clarence Irigoo. I probably don't know how to spell their names right—but I will never forget them!

More Fast Praying

A few years later, while pastoring in another Alaskan city, I received a call from the local police asking if I would be willing to come to a residence and negotiate with a lady who had barricaded herself in her house with her children and would not open up for anyone. One of the neighbors informed the police that I was her pastor, so they called me.

When I got there, the area was cordoned off by a sea of police cruisers and a big SWAT team vehicle. I was asked to go to the door and see if I could talk my way in. It seems that the lady was facing some frightening marital circumstances and she had panicked. The police said that they believed she was armed.

Well, as I walked up her sidewalk I was praying intensely under my breath that the fluttering butterfly squadrons in my stomach would calm down and God would give me wisdom. With an audience unlike any I had ever had, I began a dialogue with the woman through the door. What she could not see was that there were probably ten guns aimed at that door (with me in front of it), and two officers crouched along the side of the house just behind me. After about ten minutes, she hesitatingly cracked open the door. The two officers beside me sprang into action and grabbed her. Thankfully there were no weapons involved and the situation was diffused with no one getting hurt.

Throughout this situation there wasn't any time to bow, close my eyes or use any of the usual protocol for praying, but I am absolutely convinced that the Lord can somehow decipher our silent, rapid-fire pleas of desperation during such moments.

One More

As I expressed earlier, there are not many dull moments while serving the Lord in the land of the midnight sun because not long after the last incident, while counseling a very distraught man in a remote Alaskan area, I got another chance to do some more crisis praying. Sitting in his living room listening to him vent his rage about his situation, he suddenly sprang to his feet and walked quickly into an adjoining bedroom. "Uh-oh" was my first thought, and I hit the instant prayer mode.

When he came back out of the bedroom he had one hand behind his back. My thought was, "Uh-oh, part two . . . he has a gun back there!" Again, more prayer was sent heaven-ward in a split-second. At that moment, he moved his hand and I could see that he was holding a Bible and not a gun. He began weeping and asked me to pray with him a prayer of repentance to God for his wayward life and sins.

When it was all over and I was preparing to leave, I mentioned to him that he'd had me a little nervous there for awhile because I thought he was going to shoot me. Without blinking, he said that when he had gone to the bedroom his original intent indeed was to grab his .357 magnum handgun and do just exactly that. But when he had reached into the drawer to get the gun, his hand settled on a seldom used Bible that was also there. At that moment (while I was setting speed and sincerity records in my prayer) the Lord touched his heart and he knew that instead of committing murder, he needed to get right with God.

As I walked out into the cold fall night, miles from home, I took a moment to look up toward heaven and offer heartfelt thanks to God for his promise in Psalm 91 that the person who "dwelleth in the secret place of the most High shall abide under the shadow of the Almighty." What an incredible place to dwell. And you can get there from wherever you are—in the far north, downtown L.A., or a sandy beach on Maui.

CHAPTER 2

A Wing and a Prayer

D ue to the sheer size of Alaska (570,000 square miles) and the lack of a road system to much of the state, often the best or only way to reach your destination is to fly by small aircraft. Because of this, Alaska has by far the most private pilots per capita than any other state in the Union. So, over the years, I have been blessed to ride with some of the best "bush pilots" in the world who can take off, fly and land those little planes with more skill than most of us have in driving a car. When invited to go fly-out fishing or hunting with one of these brave souls, I have always had three basic guidelines I use in deciding whether or not to go:

1. Does this pilot love living as much as I do?
2. Does he have as many landings as he has take-offs?
3. Does he have common sense and is he aware of the sage axiom: "There are *old* pilots, and there are *bold* pilots; but there are no *old, bold* pilots?"

Yet, despite those precautions, occasionally I have wound up in situations where I found myself flying "on a wing and a prayer." Let me tell you about a few of those moments of "high adventure."

The Innoko River on Fumes

It was likely going to be one of Tom Edmondson's last hunts. Parkinson's disease had been taking its toll and even though he loved to get out into the wilderness and bring home a moose to feed his family, the tremors in his hands were starting to make it hard to hit his target. With that awareness we hooked up with a bush pilot friend and flew in his 180 Cessna on floats (pontoons) for several hours west of Anchorage past the village of McGrath to the Innoko River. The Innoko, a winding, slow-moving, coffee-colored river was known to have a good population of large bull moose, and that is what we were after.

Once we arrived to our target area, landed on the river and set up our camp, we got back in the plane and circled the area looking for moose close to camp. We saw several, landed, had dinner and then went back up for another scouting trip before crawling into our sleeping bags for the night. In Alaska, you can't hunt the same day you fly so we had to wait until dawn the next morning to begin our hunt. Sleep came hard with the anticipation of the next morning's adventure, but eventually the bubbling and hissing of the river lulled us to sleep.

Just after dawn, after walking only a few hundred yards, I spotted what looked like the roots of an up-ended tree in the high grass. Only, as I stared at it, the roots moved! It was a huge bull lying down for a nap after feeding all night. One shot and my hunt was over. A few minutes later, one of the other guys shot another one making it two monster moose to pack a quarter at a time back to our camp. The antlers on mine were 66 inches across, and the other one measured 55 inches. These were BIG animals.

Now this is where things got interesting because the pilot informed us of his concern that we might not have enough fuel to make it back to McGrath where we could fill the tanks. So, to figure out just how much fuel we did have, we drained all the fuel in both tanks into our gas cans and determined that we had 19 gallons of gas to fly fully loaded to McGrath. I was never very good at math story problems in elementary school, but being motivated to get this right, it didn't take long to confirm our pilot's concern. A 180 Cessna on floats burns roughly 16 gallons an hour and we had an hour to fly—not counting the extra fuel used under full power to take off.

Well, Tom said he would stay at camp to somewhat lessen the load and pray while I flew along with the pilot to McGrath to help with the fueling process. Knowing Tom to be a man of great faith who prayed effective prayers, that sounded like a good deal to me, so off we flew, fully loaded and with moose horns strapped to the floats. Once airborne, the pilot adjusted the throttle so that the plane was burning as lean a fuel mixture as possible. We had two mountainous areas to cross before the village and gas would come into view.

About halfway over the last mountain, suddenly the plane engine began to cough and sputter, and then it died! There is nothing quite as deafening as that kind of silence!! We were over a mountain with not a sliver of water in sight to land that rapidly descending plane. I remember distinctly what my thoughts were. First, there was anger that I'd put my life on the line for a stupid MOOSE! I don't even like moose meat that much! Never again! And, second...you know how they say that when looking death in the eye, your life flashes before your eyes? *It does.* Then, I began a quick prayer for God to PLEASE help the pilot get that plane started again. After about a minute of working the levers, the plane finally started and roared back to life. That was a wonderful sound to my ears, only surpassed by the beauty of the river that flows by McGrath when it finally came into view.

It turns out what had happened was that the pilot had leaned out the fuel mixture too far and the gas-starved engine had just died. I believe we landed with about a gallon of fuel left. Whew...and thank you, Lord! I think guardian angels stationed in Alaska deserve hazardous duty pay!!

A Bumpy but Happy Landing

Another of these airplane adventures happened while I was serving as an interim pastor in Nome. A pilot friend, who attended the church along with his wife and two sons, called one day and asked if I'd mind going along with him on a flight to the village of Elim, some miles up the coast. He was flying a twin-engine Dornier (about a 15-passenger) plane belonging to a small company, and he needed some help at the other end unloading the cargo of canned goods and a few other heavy items. Always ready for adventure, I agreed to go along for the ride and help however I could.

As we were approaching the little landing strip, loaded to the hilt, we were not aware that the local airport maintenance crew had recently plowed the bumpy snowdrifts from the runway right down to bare ice. It was a sunny spring day and the morning sun had melted some of the ice, leaving a small layer of water on top. Water on ice . . . now that is a special kind of slick!!

When the plane touched down and my friend began to apply the brakes, instead of slowing down, we seemed to pick up speed!! However, loaded too heavy to take off again, and sliding all over the super slick runway, the pilot tried a maneuver where he feathered (put in neutral) the left propeller on his side of the plane and put full power to the right side (my side) in an attempt to turn the plane 180 degrees and bring it to a stop. In theory it might have worked had the runway not had a slight decline on the end toward which we were headed.

What did happen is that the plane turned sideways and went sliding into a huge pile of snow and ice at the end of the runway at about 70 mph, ripping off the engine a few feet from my seat!!

Now, during the five to ten seconds that it took for all of this to happen, I was doing some mighty fast and honest praying. Nothing fancy about it at all—just a split second acknowledgment that we needed His help RIGHT THEN!! And, He was there just that fast. Miraculously, neither of us was injured and the plane didn't catch on fire in spite of fuel squirting all over the place from the broken fuel lines.

An interesting postlude to this story is that a few months later, my pilot friend, Kent, moved with his family to Anchorage to where we had returned also after our interim pastoring tour of duty ended. One Sunday, while his wife was visiting her family in the states, Kent attended church with me in Anchorage and accepted Christ as his Savior. Less than a week after that life-changing event in his life, Kent (flying as co-pilot this time) and several others died in a plane crash while attempting to land in a snowstorm at Happy Valley, a Trans-Alaska oil pipeline construction camp. Later that week, as I met with Kent's wife and family in Boise for his funeral, being able to share that Kent had indeed accepted Christ was a great consolation to all present.

CHAPTER 3

Adventure at 63° Below

W hen I travel to various parts of the "lower 48" states doing seminars and retreats, there are a few questions that almost always come up from inquisitive folks about life in Alaska. Do people actually live in igloos? Have I ever seen a polar bear? Is it really dark all winter long? Do I have electricity and television? But the most common question asked is *just how cold does it get up here?*

Most of the questions have simple answers. I have never seen an igloo but have read that the Alaska Native hunters in the far north used to build them as temporary shelters while on winter hunting trips. I have seen a few polar bears, but mostly on the Discovery Channel. Only in the extreme far north is it completely dark for several months in the winter. In south-central Alaska, where the majority of Alaskans live, in the dead of winter there are several hours of sunlight daily. Most populated areas of Alaska have electricity and either cable or satellite television. Even those who live in totally isolated areas will often have some sort of generator so that they can at least communicate or get news via radio.

The last question usually takes some explanation since Alaska is so geographically huge and diverse that different areas of the state have totally different climatic conditions. The Southeast and the Aleutians often have very warm and moist weather not unlike Seattle or Vancouver. South-central Alaska temperatures, while chilly in winter, are sometimes warmer than Minneapolis or the Great Lakes areas. The Interior (around Fairbanks) is a semi-arid area but can have bitter cold weather, and the furthest north area, the Arctic, can have cold and wind so severe that even the Prudhoe Bay oil operations have to restrict activity outside for periods of time.

According to the Alaska Trekker website, the coldest temperature on record was recorded at Prospect Creek, in the northern interior in 1971—80° below zero!! Br-r-r!

Just How Cold *Is* -63 Degrees?

The coldest actual temperature I have ever personally experienced was -63° in the little town of Delta Junction, near Fairbanks. I was serving as interim pastor several months during the winter of 1973 at Steese Highway Assembly of God in Fairbanks, and was also the director of The One-Way Inn, the church's outreach to the homeless. One day I received a call from the denomination's superintendent who mentioned that there was a young pastor and his family ministering a couple of hours away in Delta who could really use a visit and some encouragement.

So, we loaded a VW van with some of the One-Way Inn residents and headed up the road past a town called North Pole and on to Delta. It was about zero or thereabouts when we left Fairbanks, a fairly moderate winter afternoon. But the closer we got to Delta, it seemed to get colder by the mile. We were heading into an extreme cold front and didn't know it.

We arrived at Delta to a very warm welcome by Pastor Bob Fowler, his wife, Jessie, and their two children. We had a great time of sharing and held a church service. The incredible finale was partaking of some of Jessie's "world famous" cinnamon rolls, which were in and of themselves worthy of the drive! However, when I went outside to start up that old VW bus, the air outside nearly took my breath away. It was a special kind of *cold*. A turn of the ignition key just brought a faint "click" and no response. I hurried back inside and checked their thermometer by the door which said that it was now *63 degrees below zero*. I had often experienced zero to 30 below and occasionally had felt minus 40, but this was a biting cold that felt like icy razors cutting through the seams of my clothing. It was essential to have something over my mouth and nose to limit that cold air from going directly into my lungs.

We tried to jump-start the vehicle using one of the Fowler's cars, but that didn't do a thing. I think the oil in the VW was just too thick and cold to allow the motor to turn over. Our next bird-brained idea was to take a roasting pan, fill it with charcoal briquettes and put them under the oil pan to warm things up! Why that old VW didn't catch fire was, in reality, a bonafide miracle. Amazingly, the engine actually started! We quickly said our goodbyes, took a supply of emergency rations (the cinnamon rolls that were left), hopped in the bus and headed out the driveway. I thought we had flat tires by the clunking and wobbling of the wheels. It turns out that at those temperatures, I needed to drive very slowly for a few miles because the tires had frozen with a flat spot on one side!

It was so cold that the gas heater located in the rear of the VW could not begin to keep the windshield defrosted, so we had to keep scraping the frost off the inside of the windows. I don't recall seeing another vehicle on the road for miles until we pulled into North Pole where a sign indicated that it had warmed up to a balmy fifty below! By the time we reached Fairbanks about midnight, it felt like shirt-sleeve weather at only -30°.

Lessons Learned

There surely must be some spiritual connotations to that old lyric that "fools rush in where angels fear to tread." As I look back on that trip with a lifetime of Arctic experience now under my belt, I expect that indeed there must have been a squadron of guardian angels dressed in parkas and muk-luks (warm, skin boots worn by the Alaska Natives of the north) assigned by heaven's headquarters to keep that old VW bus and its cargo of God's kids moving safely on the road home at that temperature. With no traffic and very little emergency gear on board, a flat tire or other malfunction along the road could have been fatal. I still shake my head at the folly of venturing out on a night like that!!

The upside of the whole ordeal is that the passengers all have a tale to tell their kids and grandkids . . . and, I made a life-long friendship with the Fowlers that was forged not in the fire of adversity, but in its *icebox!*

CHAPTER 4

Alaskan Gold

A little over 100 years ago, as tales of a huge gold strike in the north spread like wildfire, thousands of hardy men and women set sail for Alaska with dreams of instant wealth! Arriving in Skagway, they packed their gear over the Chilkoot Pass to Bennett Lake where they launched their hastily built rafts and scows into the lake that eventually flowed into the mighty Yukon River, which led to the Klondike and Alaska. Eyes glazed over with "gold fever," many died along the hazardous route, while others succumbed to the harsh environment and headed back home, broke and discouraged. A precious few found their El Dorado and prospered.

It is ironic that while history records this stampede to Alaska by people *searching* for gold, today, with the mass of tourists that visit here every year, there are people coming to Alaska *bringing* their gold with them. Whether it has been the glittering gold in the ground, a tourist with his Gold American Express Card, or the "black gold" that flows through the pipeline to Valdez and out to an oil-hungry world, Alaska has always been a resource-rich, golden land of opportunity for those with the courage or obsession to go after it. I am certain that if those Russian Czars who sold Alaska to the United States for 7.2 million dollars back in 1867 knew just how valuable it would turn out to be, they would have never considered the sale. It is truly an example of how "one man's junk" turned out to be "another man's treasure."

The Real Gold

After spending most of my adult life in the land where gold or dreams of it have come and gone for so many seekers, I have determined that the "real gold" doesn't come in nuggets dug from the ground or panned from the gravel in a stream. Real Alaskan gold comes in strange packages that you might not expect.

Dandelion Gold

In most parts of the country, the arrival of the first spring dandelion in the yard is a signal for people to stampede to the nearest lawn and garden supply and load up on the stuff that is "guaranteed" to kill those nasty weeds in their tracks! In Alaska, however, after a bleak, frigid, Arctic winter has subsided, and the first dandelions start popping up in the lawn or along the roadside, sun and warmth-starved Alaskans explode into a dance of joy as they frolic in those beautiful golden yellow blossoms. Invariably, the first bouquet given to a mother, weary from having the kids indoors all winter, is a fistful of dandelions from her adventurous son or daughter! What is a pernicious weed to one person can be a source of joy or a child-like expression of love to another.

Roadside Gold Mining

The roadside along Turnagain Arm south of Anchorage is one of the first places each spring where dandelions poke their heads up. One day, while driving south on that highway toward Seward, I found the "mother lode." In a hurry to get to Seward in time to hit the incoming tide that would bring some early salmon close to shore, out of the corner of my eye I saw a car pulled off to the side of the road in a small parking area. The back hatch was open and a lone woman was standing there looking at a very flat tire. I drove on for a mile or two feeling the adrenaline begin to flow in anticipation of what I figured would be a guaranteed king salmon in the ice chest in just a few short hours.

However, invading my fishing dreams was the gnawing awareness that I really should have stopped and offered to assist that roadside traveler in distress. A mile or so more I could no longer live with my stinging conscience, so I made a quick U-turn and sped back to that pull-off. What I discovered there has made me a much richer person.

When I asked if I could help this young woman who was perhaps in her early twenties, instead of a verbal reply, she quickly fumbled through her cluttered front seat to find a little pad of paper and a pen upon which she quickly scribbled a note to me explaining that she was deaf and mute, had never changed a tire before, and was confused. I wrote her a note back saying that I used to change tires for a living and this was a "piece of cake." As I got the jack and spare out of the back of her Subaru station wagon, I heard a tiny voice behind me say, "Hello, Mister." I turned to see a little knee-high girl who had been exploring the roadside dandelion patch when I had pulled up. It turns out that this was a single mom from a little town on the Kenai Peninsula who had saved up her money and was taking her little girl to the zoo in Anchorage as their "vacation."

It didn't take long to see why she had a flat tire. The tire was balder than my aging head, with almost no tread remaining. Its mate on the other side of the car wasn't much better but was still holding air. The flat one had blown out and luckily it had happened right at that pull-out or she would have been stuck on that very narrow and dangerous road with almost no shoulders on which to park.

When the work was done, I put her flat tire in the back of her car and gave her directions to the closest tire store in Anchorage. Seeing that she obviously wasn't flush with cash I inquired (via the note pad) if she had enough money to get a couple of new tires. She jotted down that she thought she had enough and I turned to hop in my car, hoping to make up for lost time and continue to my destination. A tug on my sleeve turned me around to face this lady who extended a hastily written "thank you" note.

It was then that I saw the glitter of *pure gold*. Her little girl had picked a handful of roadside dandelions and she offered them to me as she hugged my leg! I patted her tiny head, mouthed "you're welcome" to her mom before she headed north and I headed south. I made it to the next pull-out where I had to stop, wipe the tears from my eyes and compose myself. I picked up my little bouquet of dandelions and realized the fortune that they represented.

I never learned the names of that roadside mom and her little girl, but they left me with a deposit of "real gold" that I wouldn't trade for anything, *ever!*

Eureka!

"Eureka" was the trademark verbal explosion that came from the lips of those grizzled old prospectors when they'd find "color" in the bottom of their gold pans. Many would stand guard with a loaded Winchester lest some dreaded "claim jumper" would do them in and make off with their gold. Excitement often turned to suspicion and paranoia.

With real gold, or what the Bible calls "true riches," there is no need to guard it or horde it or stash it in hidden compartments in your old cabin. True riches only increase in value when you share them or give them away. While I have a little gold coin passed on to me by Marveen's sweet Auntie Faye, and a few gold caps on some molars in my mouth, at this stage in my life I feel like a wealthy man because I have "discovered" the *real gold* in the love of my wife and family, the incredible friends who have blessed my life, and the mercy of God that has given me eternal life and allowed me to share His gift in my life with others for all these years in a place like Alaska. *Eureka, I've found it!* And I hope you have too.

CHAPTER 5

Bear Tales

You could count on it. Like clockwork at the stroke of noon, the two older gentlemen who always sat on the back row, right near the door, would stand up, put on their baseball caps, smile, and walk out of the church in Nome. It didn't matter if I was done with my sermon or not, because at noon, *they* were done with it and out into the cold they would go. While I have never been considered a "long-winded" preacher, I have been described by more than one person as an "earthy" one. "Down to earth" they say, so I generally just take it as a compliment and keep on being me. Well, another part of "me" is that I frequently enjoy good humor and sometimes try to work some of it into my sermons.

After several months of these regular but early departures by my two Inupiat parishioners, I decided that I would see if I could interest them enough in what I was saying that they might forget their lunch plans until a few minutes after noon. So, one Sunday, I decided to begin telling a true story of a bear encounter about ten minutes before twelve and drag it out for a while. I started the story and I could see they were tuned in to the tale . . . then I'd preach a little more of my sermon . . . tell a little more of the story but leave them hanging in suspense . . . then preach a little more gospel and add a few more details as the bear story built to a climax. About ten minutes *after* noon, one of them looked down at his watch, poked his buddy, and the two of them stood, put on their hats and headed for the door. But not before one of them turned, grinned, shook a finger at me and walked out the door.

The next Sunday, during the traditional greeting time before the sermon, I approached one of the early departers, and as he shook my hand he smiled and said, "You got me! How did that story end, anyway?" We both had a good laugh as I told him the finale.

While that story-telling experience was comical, a real encounter with one of Alaska's undisputed heavyweight champions of the north is usually *not* a joking matter at the time. While they may appear to be cuddly little balls of fur that you'd like to pet and feed, in reality they can be incredibly vicious and can tear a man or animal limb from limb in a heartbeat. I cringe when I hear of someone who goes out into bear country armed with a whistle or a can of pepper spray! While jokes abound about human-bear encounters, if you are ever in close proximity with a huge bear that can snap a 1,000-pound moose's neck with one blow, rise up on his hind legs and stand ten to twelve feet high and cover a hundred yards in around five seconds, joke if you will. But I generally go prepared to defend myself if need be.

Skiing on Snowshoes

One early spring afternoon, in 1972, while hunting on

snowshoes for ptarmigan (members of the grouse family) on Diamond Ridge near Homer, I had one of those encounters that probably contributed some to the gray hair I now have. I had seen a flock of birds fly around a small but thick stand of spruce trees to an adjacent stretch of willow bushes, so I decided to sneak through the woods (a challenge on snow-shoes in the deep snow) and see if I could shoot a couple with my .22 caliber rifle. Ptarmigan, by the way, are excellent table fare if prepared correctly.

Well, as I was creeping through the brush, being careful not to step on any branches that might snap and give away my strategy to the cagey birds, I suddenly heard a low grunting sound that made me freeze in mid-step. I had been so intent on watching the ground and not making noise that I didn't realize I had walked to within thirty feet of an upturned spruce tree—under which was a bear den. Sitting on its haunches at the entrance to its den was a huge brown bear! It was a rela-tively warm and sunny day and while there were still several feet of snow remaining on the ground, he had decided to come out for a late-hibernation stretch.

As I began to inch my way backwards in my snowshoe tracks, he evidently caught my human scent and growled a deep and angry sounding growl that sent my heart pounding in my chest and chills down my spine. He did not sound happy to be interrupted in his bedroom! I had a .300 Weatherby rifle slung over my backpack, but didn't want to make any excess movement in my retreat. By the way, have you ever tried to walk backwards in snowshoes? It is a challenge for a rookie not to get tangled up even while walking forwards! I had instant visions of this cranky bear, hungry and sore from sleeping all winter, making a charge at me with the intent of having me for his Easter dinner!

So, praying silently as I backed up, I made it to the place where I had entered the thicket. Then, in one motion, I spun around and began running, almost skiing as fast as I could on those snowshoes back toward the safety of my truck. Thankfully, he must have been too groggy to mount a chase and probably went back to bed thinking he'd just had a bad dream! As for me, I stopped by the grocery store on the way home and got chicken for dinner!

Yes, God's Love Takes Good Care of Me

Later that summer, I decided to hike into the back-country and fish the headwaters of the Anchor River (also near Homer) in hopes of catching a few of the big rainbow trout that remain in the remote reaches of that beautiful stream. I had the whole river to myself that day. Well, at least I knew of no other people around there.

I had been having a great time enjoying the beauty of Alaska and catching and releasing fish after fish and somehow allowed myself to momentarily forget that this was also prime bear country. Until . . . I suddenly detected a really foul-smelling odor in the air. I looked around to see if there were any dead salmon carcasses nearby and could see none. Now, one habit that bears have is that they occasionally will roll in the remains of a rotting salmon. I guess it is their version of nice smelling cologne. I was standing on one side of a chest-high willow patch probably the size of a tennis court. Out of the corner of my eye I saw movement in the bushes. Then I discovered what I had been smelling as a huge brown bear stood up on his hind legs to investigate that strange odor he had smelled! It was human scent and it was me!

Another characteristic of bears is that they can smell much better than they can see, so I ducked down and in the same motion unslung my rifle from my shoulder and clicked the safety to the off position. Armed and on full alert, I peeked up over the willows to assess the situation just as this huge bear opened his mouth, roared and snapped his jaws (one of an angry bear's warning signals). I have to tell you, that sound is not what you might expect of an animal smacking his chops together. It sounded to me like a builder slapping two pieces of 2x4 wood together!

Pow!

Hearing that sound and knowing the raw power it represented, the rifle in my hands suddenly seem to shrink and feel more like a pea shooter. And it felt like the electricity in my nervous system was creating a whole new set of neuro-pathways to my fight or flight system. In this case, the *flight* response seemed the most appropriate and I made a hasty retreat leaving this big bear to fish that spot all by himself.

Downstream and out of sight and sound of one of Alaska's most majestic but fearsome critters, an old song we often sang in church came to me, I began whistling the tune to "Yes, God's Love Takes Good Care of Me." It had new meaning that day. I am always thankful for God's loving protection, even when we blunder into places where guardian angels put in overtime.

CHAPTER 6

Lake Clark— A Wilderness Oasis

For about five years during the 90s I made an annual trip to the tiny community of Port Alsworth on the shores of Lake Clark. My good friends, Dr. Jerry Coles and his wife, Beckie, maintained a summer residence there (a sturdy vinyl tent on a wood platform), and generally around the first week of July, when the sockeye salmon started to arrive, Jerry would call to see if I was free to make the 100-mile flight southwest of Anchorage with him. We would usually fish for grayling on Friday night where small feeder streams dumped into the emerald green waters of Lake Clark, and then fish for sockeye salmon on Saturday where the Tazimina River emptied into adjoining Six-Mile Lake across from the village of Nondalton. I'd always wrap up the trip by preaching at Tanalian Bible Church in Port Alsworth before flying back to Anchorage on Sunday afternoon.

It was a highlight of my summer to get away from the crowds and experience this absolutely gorgeous piece of

Alaska. Just the flight there through the jaws of Lake Clark Pass with its huge peaks, glaciers and glacial river deltas is impressive beyond words. While silt-laden glacial water enters the 110-square-mile Lake Clark at its northern end, most of the water in the rivers and creeks that empty into the lake is so clear that it is almost like fishing in liquid glass. Watching an 18" grayling torpedo up from the bottom of a pool to slam into your fly is a rare treat for any fisherman.

Rural Governor's Mansion

Besides the awesome fishing and scenery, Lake Clark was the home of former governor, Jay Hammond, who recently passed away. Governor Hammond was a much loved and respected leader in Alaska and he somehow managed to keep his rural Alaskan roots intact in spite of all the political pressures his office required. The title of his last book referred to him as Alaska's Bush Rat Governor, a comical but respected nick-name in Alaska. It was not unusual to run into him at Peggy's Café near Merrill Field in Anchorage, sitting on a stool at the counter wearing his wool shirt and suspenders while eating a piece of pie before hopping in his plane to head back to his log cabin on Lake Clark.

On one of our Friday night grayling fishing trips, Jerry pulled his boat close to the shoreline in front of the Governor's house to see if he were there, but the absence of their plane at the dock let us know that nobody was home. I had met him on numerous occasions and was disappointed that I wouldn't be able to hear the latest poem he'd either written or memorized. Where else on this planet can you feel free to pull up beside the former governor's house in a boat and, if he is home, have a good chance of being invited in for a cup of coffee?

The Salmon Invasion

One year our visit to the Tazimina River to fish for sockeye (red) salmon looked to be a bust because the salmon were late in arriving. We fished for grayling for awhile and sat in the boat and swatted the clouds of mosquitoes while we ate lunch and made plans to head back to Port Alsworth. Just before casting off, we found ourselves suddenly surrounded by jumping salmon. The fish had arrived and it was a sight to behold. They came in waves of hundreds and thousands as their inner guidance system led them to their home stream to spawn. We managed to hook and land a few of these ocean fresh fish, but the real thrill was just being there to witness their mass arrival.

Ahh . . . Cool, Clear, Water!

On our ride back to Port Alsworth, the afternoon sun was hot on the glassy smooth water. The temperature felt to be close to ninety. As we skimmed along at full throttle, I noticed what looked like two big upended stumps along the shoreline, perhaps ten yards out into the lake. Neither of us remembered them being there before so we veered toward the shore for a closer look. When we got to within two or three-hundred yards from shore, our "stumps" stood up and trotted into the woods. What we thought were tree stumps turned out to be two huge bull moose, in full velvet, that had decided the best way to cool off from the heat and escape the mosquitoes and flies was to just go sit down in the cold waters of the lake. If we'd had time, I think I would have joined them for a swim.

Eagles Can Swim

On another Friday night grayling fishing trip, as we passed a little cove, I noticed some splashing in the water about thirty feet offshore. We pulled the boat closer to investigate and discovered a mature bald eagle splashing in the water with its wings. As we watched, this majestic bird began to use his wings in sort of a butterfly stroke in the water to propel himself to the shore. I had never witnessed such a sight, and when the eagle reached shore, he hopped out of the water with a huge lake trout (maybe fifteen pounds) securely locked in the grip of his talons. Evidently the trout was too heavy for the eagle to carry and still get airborne. With no solid ground under the fish so the eagle could dislodge its talons, it was forced to swim for shore or drown with the fish. By flapping his wings and hopping, he managed to drag the fish a few yards ashore and up on a log where he began a dinner of lake trout sushi.

One Last Surprise

In what turned out to be my last trip to Port Alsworth, I was asked to do my usual Sunday morning sermon. I remember being blessed not to have to don a suit and tie since a tee shirt, jeans and tennis shoes were standard clergy attire in this casual environment. Besides, a suit crammed into a duffel bag along with my hip waders and fishing gear would definitely not travel "wrinkle free." Along with Pastor James Walsh and his young family and Dr. Coles, there was an eclectic assortment of folks in attendance ranging from local sourdoughs, bush pilots, summer vacationers and workers from the Tanalian Bible Camp that was gearing up for another session of summer camp.

During my sermon I noticed a tall, lanky man in the back wearing sunglasses, but I didn't recognize him. After the service and after praying for a few folks with needs that my sermon had addressed, Jerry asked me if I knew who that big guy in the back was. Responding to my negative reply, he informed me that it was Franklin Graham, son of Billy Graham, one of the world's most respected and fruitful evangelists and preachers. Upon learning that information, I remember saying to Jerry, "Holy cow! If I'd known I was preaching with him in the audience, I'd have really been nervous!" But he just looked like another fisherman to me.

I think about that Lake Clark experience now and then when I am preaching to our congregation in Nikiski and wonder if perhaps I am preaching to the *next* Billy Graham or another future great evangelist. Only God knows for sure.

CHAPTER 7

Carharts, Bunny Boots, and the Kingdom of God

Alaska is a big, harsh land, and the people who call it home most generally do so because they *want* to live here and have come to terms with the climate, long hours of winter darkness, and bone chilling cold. While Anchorage, Fairbanks, and a few other cities are modern cosmopolitan areas not unlike what you might find in what we call the "lower 48", there are few other places in the world where you can find moose in your backyard, watch the northern lights from your porch, or, in the summer, go fishing at midnight and need sunglasses. But it is the people themselves that make Alaska the place I have kept calling home for most of my adult life. Let me give you a few little slices of life on the last frontier to show you what I mean.

Ditch Diving on a Wintry Day

One year in early January, while driving with my wife, Marveen, down to Juneau where she would be spending the next five months working for the legislature (her job for 13 years), the weather took a particularly nasty turn creating very hazardous driving conditions. It is about an 800-mile trip from Anchorage to Haines, and then a ferry ride for several hours to the dock at Auke Bay, a few miles from Juneau and the Capitol Building.

As we rounded one very sharp corner near the town of Tok, Alaska, we noticed a car in the ditch and several people standing along the roadway. We recognized them as some of Marveen's fellow legislative staffers who were also on their annual trek to Juneau for the session. We pulled over to see if we could be of help and noticed one hard-working man off the road, where the marooned car was, digging and tossing snow in every direction. He reminded me of a dog looking for a buried bone. I was impressed with how hard he was working and I assumed by the way he was dressed (Carhart coveralls, white bunny boots and a stocking hat) that he was a local sourdough who had a big heart and had stopped to render assistance to these hapless city folks.

Then, suddenly the man with the shovel popped up out of the snow, pulled off his stocking hat to mop his brow and said, "Howdy Wayne, how's it goin'!" It was none other than then State Representative Mark Hanley, a very respected legislator and, at the time, co-chair of the influential House Finance Committee. What a pleasant surprise to find someone of his stature who was willing to roll up his sleeves, get down in a ditch and tackle a hard, sweaty job. It reminded me of the "good Samaritan" story in the Bible where the Samaritan man was willing to go out of his way simply to be kind to someone in need.

While I already had great respect for Rep. Hanley, my esteem for him grew greatly that snowy afternoon along the Alaska Highway. He would make a great governor.

Sid the Kid

Just about anyone who has been a resident of Anchorage for very long has probably heard of or met Sid the Kid—a nickname for part time pastor, part time welder, iron worker and salvage yard owner, Sid Glasscock. Sidney (as his wife calls him), is truly what I call a "colorful Alaskan." Always ready with a joke, word of encouragement and a ready smile, Sid happens to be one of the kindest and biggest-hearted men in the great land of Alaska. Little kids, grizzled truckers, tottering grannies and homeless street people alike have all been blessed by this gentle giant.

On one occasion Sid and his sweet wife, Carol (a very talented artist whose shop is called Junk Yard Art by Carol), ventured out in the middle of a frigid rainy October night to tow my old Volvo with a blown head gasket 60 miles one way back to Anchorage. When they arrived at the scene of the Volvo's demise, Sid hopped out of his wrecker, hobbled over to where we were standing, gave me a big hug and hollered, "Hey Wayne-O, lets get this wounded pup back to town!" Two hours later, safe, sound and dry back in Anchorage, he would not hear of taking money for his act of love and friendship. A pretty rare fellow, this Sid the Kid.

Now, on any wintry day in Alaska, you can usually spot Sid walking from a mile away, partly because his hard life has left his body pretty beaten and worn and he walks with a distinct hitch and a limp from bad knees, hips, back and ankles. But even more predictable would be his uniform. He wears some old, very worn (broken in well) Carhart overalls and those white bubble-toed "bunny boots" that I think were invented by the military to keep its Arctic soldiers from getting frostbite on their toes.

If you don't know what Carharts and bunny boots are, this story won't have as much meaning for you. But suffice it to say, you probably won't find them hanging on the high fashion racks at any upscale boutiques in Hollywood or New York. While they will never win fashion awards, these garments are practical and functional for hard working, blue-collar workers in professions that require outside work in very cold or adverse conditions. They are kind of like an old salvage barge or tug boat in the shipyards—not much to look at, but if you need a rescue or a tow to shore, they are just what you need.

The Kingdom of God Is . . .

When you stop to think about it, guys like Mark and Sid and their trademark working clothes speak something to us of God's values and His kingdom. In Galatians 6:2-3, the Bible (Amplified Version) encourages us to "Bear (endure, carry) one another's burdens *and* troublesome moral faults . . . For if any person thinks himself to be somebody (too important to condescend to shoulder another's load), when he is nobody (of superiority except in his own estimation), he deceives *and* deludes *and* cheats himself." Evidently God isn't all that impressed with our fancy clothing and degrees, titles and reputations, but He does place a great value on our being willing to take a bucket of water, bar of soap and an old bath towel, and wash the feet of those who need them washed! The Kingdom of God and its grandeur is seen clearly in love that is pure, humble, and simple and gets the job done.

One day, during a very difficult time in my life, Sid the Kid came up to me, put his big arm on my shoulder, looked me in the eye and said, "Wayne, I want to be your friend. I probably won't be a very good one, but I want to be your friend." I took him up on his offer, and an incredible friend he has been. In my book, Sid the Kid is a big man in God . . . and I could care less if he wears those faded and torn old Carharts and dorky looking bunny boots!!

CHAPTER 8

Circuit Riding Preacher on a Horse Named Honda

As a young boy, I remember reading an old paperback book entitled *The Fighting Parson of the Old West* (Bernard Palmer, Wm. B. Eerdmans Publishing Co., 1942). It was an exciting tale that described the exploits of a circuit riding preacher who would stand up for what was right while preaching a straight-from-the-hip message to a rugged and often lawless group of ranchers, rustlers, homesteaders, gunslingers and gamblers. I would often imagine that I'd been born a hundred years earlier and I was one of those circuit riding preachers taking the gospel to the Old West.

Then, a few years back, while my wife and I were on a trip through some of the eastern states, we decided to by-pass the interstate highways and take smaller back roads from the Washington, D.C. area to Ohio. What we discovered was that almost all of those small, non-descript towns and villages had typically a general store, gas station, mom and pop cafe, post office and a United Methodist Church dating back to the "olden days" when one circuit riding parson made pastoral visits between a number of these little hamlets on his trusty horse.

In my mind's eye, I could easily envision the lanky old preacher swinging down out of the saddle, brushing off the trail dust, reaching into his saddle bags to retrieve his weather worn Bible, and striding through the front door of the church to find the little congregation gathered and waiting for his arrival. I could hear his spurs jingling as he walked down the center aisle with long, purposeful strides. Then, after surveying the group before him, he would offer a short and sincere prayer, open his Bible and get down to business preaching the sermon he had mulled over and over in his mind on the long ride there. No pretense. No pomp or protocol. Just simply preaching the Word and laying a spiritual foundation in the lives of people, a spirituality which has been passed down from generation to generation and still lives today.

Fast forward now to the late 1980s when the Lord opened some doors of ministry for us in the colorful Alaskan town of Seward, a small fishing and tourist oriented town some 120 miles southwest of Anchorage. Pastoring this little church was a wonderful blessing and we grew to really love the folks who were a part of it. Early in the ministry, part of the package was a twice a week commute to Seward from our home in Anchorage through some pretty awful weather conditions from time to time.

Later there were some Sundays when my preaching assignments would have us leaving Anchorage very early in order to preach in Talkeetna, 120 miles north of Anchorage only to drive like crazy to be in Seward, 120 miles to the south of Anchorage in time for the evening service while logging about 500 miles on our car for the day. We loved the drive . . . well, most of the time.

In early 1991, the old Volvo that I had been driving developed some terminal problems and a new car was needed. After considerable prayer about the situation, the Lord miraculously provided the means to pay cash for a brand new 1991 Honda Accord. It was a fiery red beauty, and I laughingly began calling myself the "circuit riding preacher on a horse named Honda." Ten years and 280,000 trouble free miles later, my trusty steed blew a cylinder and head gasket while in Colorado.

I had just about decided to sell the old gal for what I could get for her when a good friend (who had participated in the purchase of the car in the first place) called and offered to drive 2,200 miles round trip to tow the wounded warrior to Texas where his mechanic would put in a good used engine for a very reasonable price. Now, back in Alaska and with over 335,000 miles on the rest of her systems, she is still faithfully carrying us to ministry opportunities without a glitch.

One winter night while returning to Anchorage from Seward, I found myself driving in an unusually nasty wind and rainstorm. Rain on already icy roads makes for tricky driving at best. With little other traffic on the road, and the wind at my back, I was able to cruise along safely at about 50 mph. However, on several occasions I could see and feel the strong gusts of wind blowing sheets of rain past me like I was sitting still. It really got my attention when the wind (gusting at 90 mph I later learned) caught the back of my car and began pushing the back end clockwise around to the front!! With a cliff on one side and the churning iceberg-filled waters of Turnagain Arm on the other, sliding sideways like a crab at 50 mph was not my idea of fun.

A person learns a new depth of sincere prayer in moments like those. I doubt those old circuit riding preachers had to contend with such hazards; rather they faced things like bandits, a lame horse or an occasional rattlesnake coiled in the trail. Yet God is ever faithful.

A few nights ago I hopped in the little red Honda in my current home in Nikiski and pointed her toward Seward once again. It was another of those wild and wacky winter nights when it was raining on ice along the coast and snowing and blowing wet snow in the mountains. Almost like a horse that can find its way home even on the darkest of nights, the Honda plowed through the elements and returned me safely home to Nikiski just before midnight. As I parked the car in the garage, I had a peculiar feeling like I should take her saddle off, rub her down and give her a fresh bag of oats for the night. Instead, I patted her hood and said a prayer of thanks to God for one more safe trip as a "circuit riding preacher on a horse named Honda!"

$trutz'$ Chicken

My old friend, pastor and neighbor, Dick Strutz, used to fancy himself a city farmer and couldn't help himself when those cute little chickens and ducks would go on sale at the feed store every spring. We lived for a few years on Strutz Avenue in the Anchorage foothills and could always tell it was getting close to fishing season in the spring because he'd be working on his boat, planting a garden and occasionally raising poultry.

Well, one year, back in the mid-eighties, during a time when we were in the midst of beginning a new church in Anchorage, since we didn't have an office or church building yet, some of the elders and pastors would meet at Dick's house several mornings a week to pray together, line out our goals, and then head out into the city to spend time with the folks in the congregation.

It was during one of these early morning sessions, while thinking and praying, I looked out a window on Dick's chicken-wire pen in which he had about a dozen chickens and ducks. He had just fed them and they were all lined up along a trough feeding on a line of cracked corn. It reminded me a lot of my years growing up on our little farm in northwest Washington where chickens were always more enjoyable when it was someone else's responsibility to clean up after them.

Well, a few days later when we arrived for our morning gathering, I noticed a big husky-mix dog was tied up to a tree out front and was looking a little the worse for wear. We quickly learned that this stray mutt had broken into the chicken/duck compound and had eaten all but one chicken and a few of the ducks. Oh, Yuk. Can you imagine a belly full of chicken feathers and raw chicken, innards and all? I'd look peaked too! When I looked down on the chicken/duck pen, what I saw wasn't pretty. There were feathers everywhere and the critters were lined up along the feed trough for their breakfast. The ducks were all trying to feed, but the lone chicken was walking up and down in the middle of the trough causing the ducks to angrily nip and peck at him wherever he wandered.

This harassment had evidently been going on for some time because that poor lonely chicken had almost no feathers left except for a tuft or two on its tail. I actually felt sorry for that forlorn little guy...without a friend in its whole world. I wished I could tape a few feathers back on his naked little body but, sadly, I figured his days as a featherless chicken were numbered.

"A friend in need ... "

By the next prayer-time at Dick's house, I was anxious to see if "chicken little" had survived. It was raining one of those cold, bone-chilling and bordering on snow, spring-time rains in Anchorage, and I thought there would be nothing but ducks left at the grain trough. What I saw is still tattooed in my mind. It was raining so hard that instead of feeding, the ducks were huddled together under a shelter that Dick had made from a sheet of corrugated metal to protect his little flock from the pelting rain. I scanned the pen for a glimpse of the chicken and didn't see him at first. Then I saw him, huddled up close and almost under a wing of one of the female ducks. With that driving rain bouncing off the roof of their little shelter, the chicken had finally found an ally, a friend in court, a place of comfort and safety.

I don't want to get melodramatic about this, but I actually got tears in the corner of my eyes as I saw this scene unfold, and immediately that verse popped into my mind about Jesus being our advocate with the Father, interceding for us (1 Jn. 2:1).

Strategic Allies

It is a fact of life that all of us, at one time or another, wind up in the crossfire of life and become acutely aware that we *really* do need one another. Misguided though he was, Peter took up a sword in defense of his friend and Master, Jesus, when he was being betrayed and arrested. Paul had Barnabas come to his defense when none of the other disciples trusted the validity of this former death squad leader's new-found faith. David had Jonathan stand by him when Saul was on the warpath. And, Moses had two allies stand with him, holding his arms up when the battle depended on it.

Mutual Vulnerability

I love the story in 1 Samuel 18 where, as a sign of their loyalty to one another, Jonathan gave David his robe, his *sword and his bow*. By this act, he made himself vulnerable to another man. And by disarming himself he gave David the ability to do him harm if he chose. In reality, there was mutual vulnerability because, since David trusted Jonathan, it would have been a simple matter for Jonathan to set a trap for David and deliver him into the hands of Saul and his jealousy-driven murderous intentions.

My "spiritual father," Warren Carlsen, used to preach powerfully on how much Paul valued his friend, Onesiphorus (2 Timothy 1:16, NIV). It says that his friend "... often refreshed me and was not ashamed of my chains." Paul goes on to say that even when he was in prison and many had deserted him, Onesiphorus eagerly sought him out and visited him.

It is often in those bleak times in our lives, like the featherless chicken, when our true friends and allies come and stand beside us with words of encouragement.

It also encourages me when I read the account where the apostle Paul was stoned and left for dead under a pile of rocks. The Bible says that his comrades in the gospel gathered around him and began to pray for him. When I let my imagination go and put myself into Paul's shoes, I can feel him fighting his way out of unconsciousness, battered, bloody, and probably with a horrendous headache, hearing one of his friends say, "Come on Paul, wake up! You can make it. You can do it. Don't quit." And as they began removing those layers of stones and his bruised body began to stir, a shout of joy rang out from his friends as the old warrior stood on wobbly legs and probably said through his tears, "Thank you, my brothers and sisters. I guess I said something to make those bad guys mad! So, take me to the ship, I have places to go and people to see on behalf of the Master!"

I have mentioned a few of my own allies in other places in this book. There are more ... life-saving friends and family who have a habit of showing up when the rest of the world seems to have beaten a hasty retreat. They know who they are. I know who they are. God knows them well. And, I owe my life and ministry to them. Thanks for not being "ashamed of my chains."

CHAPTER 10

Homer, Hippies, and Dogs

How I ever wound up in Homer in the early 70s was a mystery to me. I had just been in Alaska a few months when I got a call from a church in Homer (at the end of the road on the Kenai Peninsula) asking if I was interested in driving down and preaching for them that Sunday, and, if I did well, they might be interested in hiring me as their pastor. Being dirt poor and with a car that was only marginally functional, we decided to borrow a decent car and drive the five hours from Anchorage to Homer to give it a whirl.

As I recall, there were about thirteen people present and, after giving my best two sermons (I had three or four then in my total arsenal) they held a brief meeting and offered me the job. Our housing was an apartment in the basement of the church, and my starting salary was fifty dollars per week and all the fish I could catch! The following week, we packed all our belongings into our old car and headed to Homer. At the edge of town, the car quit. So, with our daughter, Tracie, riding on my shoulders and infant, Michele, in her mother's arms, we walked into town for my first assignment as a "senior" pastor.

I remember our first Sunday . . . hardly a soul showed up. It turns out that it was the opening weekend of the king salmon fishing season, and anyone able-bodied enough to fish was at the river!

I have to tell you, even though Homer is literally at the *end* of the road and at that time had no paved streets, there certainly are worse places to wind up as a rookie pastor. It is absolutely beautiful! Located on pristine Kachemak Bay, mountains coming right down to the sea, the unique Homer Spit (a 4.5 mile appendix of land jutting out into the bay), glaciers, and volcanoes are all visible at the same time. I had to pinch myself to grasp the reality that I was now living in a place that would be my number one choice in the world to spend a vacation.

But with hungry kids to feed I couldn't just stand and gawk at the scenery, so I got right to it and landed three part-time jobs to augment my church salary. I was cleaning the Fish & Game offices, stocking shelves at the drug store, and pumping gas at Sunny Service. Life was busy but there were times when I would head down to the bay and catch my limit of six coho (silver) salmon on my lunch break!

As I mentioned earlier, at that time Homer had no paved roads, so dust and mud were a part of life. The high point of our week was often the arrival of the weekly produce truck bringing fresh fruit from Anchorage. Ah-h . . . for at least a few days we had fresh bananas, grapes and oranges to stave off scurvy! With a big freezer in the church, we actually dined well on shrimp, crab, halibut, salmon and moose. Occasionally one of the commercial fishermen in the community would drop off a garbage bag full of big prawns, and one time we came home to find a 75-pound halibut deposited in our shower! This was fun.

And slowly but surely our little congregation began to grow.

Here Come the Hippies

One of the memorable social phenomena of the 60s was the "hippie" culture that grew out of the West Coast, and by the early 70s some of those young people had begun to work their way to the last frontier where they could still find a cheap piece of property on which to build a cabin or tepee and "live off the land." Homer, at the end of the road, was where many of them ended their journey. It was not unusual to have a half-dozen or more of them show up on any given day at the door of our basement apartment wanting to know if they could stay awhile, have a shower, do their laundry, and eat our food until they got on their feet. Most found jobs in local canneries for the summer and by fall had either headed south for the winter or found a place to live in the woods.

Molly

I will never forget a young lady named Molly, who showed up at our door one day having hitch-hiked with her backpack and dog all the way from Boston to Homer. She was an attractive gal sporting pig-tails, a red bandana, bib-overalls, and . . . was smoking a corncob pipe. Life was never dull, and because we had not learned to say "no" to anyone in need or to set decent boundaries, we opened our church, home and empty Sunday school rooms upstairs to most all comers. It was this season of life when I learned to be a pretty decent fisherman, out of self-defense, in order to feed all of our "guests." What we did not know was that the "hippie underground network" was at work, and word had spread far and wide that if you ever made it to Homer, you could "crash" at our house!

Church Growth—Homer Style

One of the first of these modern day nomads to begin attending the church was a young woman who lived about thirty miles east of Homer at the "head of the bay" with her boyfriend *in a tent*. Yes, they lived year-round in a wall tent fully equipped with a wood floor and a stove while they worked the land with horses. Once you got to the end of the gravel road, it was a long walk several miles up and down the ridges through bear country to their "house."

Well, as the story goes, she'd gotten up early one frosty morning to put a kettle on the stove to warm some water for tea. Their honey jar was empty so she put a five-gallon can of bulk honey on the edge of the stove to warm up to pouring temperature. Her boyfriend was away so she just hopped back under the covers to catch a few more winks of sleep while things warmed up. When she awakened, she realized that she had forgotten to loosen the lid on the honey container, and its sides were bowed out from the now warm and expanded contents. Without thinking, she hurriedly loosened the top and— blurp!—the honey shot into the air and covered her and the tent floor with warm, sticky, honey! Clearing her eyes, she had no alternative but to head up the trail to the nearest shower (miles away) at the Rainwater's (known for their hospitality) house at the trailhead.

I am one of those guys who simply can't stand "sticky" fingers. A wood floor with sticky honey on it would have driven me nuts. So, when I heard the story, I gathered up a bunch of carpet remnants that we had at the church, put them in a backpack and hauled them down the trail to put on the floor to cover up the "sticky" until spring when it would warm up enough to deal with it. That was how I met Mike and Sherry. It was a few months later that they decided that just "living together" wasn't the right thing to be doing, and I had the honor of performing my first Alaskan wedding.

I will never forget Mike and Sherry standing before me with a crowd of hippies gathered in the church. Mike, (all 6'10" of him) dressed in his best rubber boots, logger pants with red suspenders and floppy felt hat . . . and Sherry, in her flowered dress standing at about 5-feet even! When it came time for Mike to kiss the bride, he just picked her up and lifted her up to smoochin' height and did the honors to a cheering audience! I love Alaska.

J. C. & Company

It was about this time when we decided that we'd invite an Anchorage-based Christian rock and roll band to come to Homer to see if perhaps some of our new friends could be enticed to become followers of Jesus. After a few weeks of putting the word out on the street (there was only one!) and into the woods, the night of the concert finally arrived and J. C. & Company cranked up their amplifiers and let'er rip for Jesus to a full house. The old-timers who attended plugged their ears, wincing in pain, but the hippies loved it and kept clapping and cheering for more.

At the end of their performance, the group's wild, frizzy-haired evangelist gave an invitation for those interested in accepting Jesus to come forward and kneel at some benches placed along the front of the church. One by one a good number came. It was awesome. Then, my defining moment as a young pastor came when Molly, the Bostonian hippie, made her way to the front of the church, accompanied by her little black spaniel-type dog she'd smuggled in with her for the concert. Molly knelt, folded her hands and began to pray, asking the Lord to come into her heart. And, (this is the honest truth) right beside her, her little dog sat up, put his paws up on the bench, and rested his chin on them as if to join in with Molly's special moment.

News Travels Fast

I can't tell you how fast the news of that event spread through that quiet little seaside town of Homer, that even the "dogs were getting saved at that hippie church!" Frankly, I did not care then, nor do I now, if someone brings their dog with them to make an eternal decision for Christ, but that moment was flash frozen into my legacy as a pastor at the end of the road.

Several years later, after we had relocated to the "big city" of Anchorage, I ran into the man who had taken my place as the pastor. In his distinct Louisiana drawl, he shook his head and lamented, ". . . Brother Wayne, there are two things I can't stand about Homer because of you, hippies and dawgs!" It seems that it took quite awhile for the word to filter out that we had left and that the free place to stay in Homer was no longer quite as available. And, the town historians who gathered around the big table at the Hotel Café to philosophize every Wednesday still loved to re-tell the tale of the night that the dog got saved!

My successor did allow, however, that the nice two-seater outhouse in the bushes behind the church that I had converted to a smokehouse was a novel idea. It had been donated by yet another young hippie gal whose cabin had burned to the ground. She was so discouraged that she decided to move back to San Francisco. She figured that the outhouse was too nice a structure to just sit unused on her abandoned cabin site. Those were the days!

CHAPTER 11

Don't Take the Bait

I t was early autumn and the sun was still hiding behind those darkest hours before the dawn when I left the house in Homer and drove the twenty miles to one of my favorite little steelhead trout fishing streams, Stariski Creek, to try my luck. The fireweed had already run its blossoms to the top of the stalks and there was a slight chill in the air. Parking by an unmarked trail (known only by local guys), I slung my rifle over my shoulder, applied some mosquito spray, grabbed my pole and headed into the woods with that familiar adrenaline rush that comes with going fishin'.

Another Day in Paradise

Daylight was just coming to the northland as I began my trek up and down a few ravines and over some dead trees that had fallen across the old trail. After seeing a few piles of fresh bear scat, I paused long enough to chamber a shell into my .338 magnum Winchester, just in case I might startle a brown bear and have to fire a warning shot.

My destination was the last bend of the creek before it headed out into a high, grassy tidal area. An average high tide would back the creek water up to right where I was intending to fish. There was a huge (maybe 7' high) boulder that stood guard over a beautiful and fairly deep pool that ran along the clay base of the bluff overlooking Cook Inlet. Being as quiet as I could, I leaned up against the boulder and peeked around it to see if any fish had come in on the previous night's high tide. My eyes widened and my pulse quickened as I counted a school of around thirty, chrome-sided, ocean-fresh, steelhead lined up like soldiers on parade. For a die-hard steelhead fisherman, this was about as good as it gets.

No Need to Yell, "Fish On!"
(When you are the only person there!)

Not wanting to spook the fish, I quickly baited my single bare hook with a big cluster of home-cured salmon eggs (legal to use in those days), peeled some line off my reel and, without exposing my presence, softly lobbed the bait over the rock. With a "*splat*," it landed just upstream of the waiting cadre of fish, where it slowly sank and began a slow bounce along the bottom. I carefully watched the movement of the line, knowing it was drifting into the path of those waiting fish. Suddenly, it just stopped. Not having any sinker on the line, I knew that if the line stopped, odds were it was because a fish was sampling breakfast, so I jerked sharply backward on my old classic fiberglass Fenwick fly rod and felt the hook hit something solid.

I quickly stepped out from behind the boulder just as a large silver steelhead exploded out of the water like a rodeo bull out of the chute. The other fish were scurrying in all directions and the big female steelhead on the end of my line danced on its tail from one end of the pool to the other. (The females tend to jump when hooked, whereas the males sulk and brood on the bottom)

About ten-minutes later, she laid on her side in the shallows, gleaming in the morning sun, a vanquished foe. Now, at the time, the limit was two fish per day and I was raised on the Skagit River in Washington State to appreciate the fine taste of fresh steelhead cooked on a grill, fried, smoked or baked. I loved it. But somehow, that morning and at that moment, I just couldn't bring myself to whack that beautiful fish and end its life. I am not a died-in-the-wool "catch and release" fisherman, and especially so when I had a wife and kids at home for whom to provide. But this moment was something special. So, I removed the hook gently from her jaw, revived her, and slowly set her free to rejoin her regiment that had disappeared into the shadows.

Then, I leaned back on that boulder, smiled to myself, and soaked up the ambience of the moment . . . grateful to be alive, healthy, and able to enjoy such an incredible moment. My dad, who fished for steelhead every winter in Washington, would have loved being there with me that day.

I hope I was able to effectively paint that morning for you with words, because, over thirty years later, I can still see the fall colors and dark waters of Stariski Creek, smell the highbush cranberries along the trail, and remember that "peaceful easy feeling." Times have changed now and virtually all steelhead fishing is "catch and release" in Alaska and the use of bait on the hook is not allowed. While these wily fish can be tricked into biting fake fish eggs or fuzzy bug-like offerings, it was sure easier to catch them with egg protein that they ate for their first meal as they were hatching.

"Don't Take the Bait!"

Nowadays, I occasionally conduct group sessions to help folks deal with anger issues in their lives. One of the props I use to make a point is a big, bright-colored fishing lure called a "Spin-n-Glo" with a huge hook attached that fishermen often use to catch king salmon on the Kenai River. I hold it up and blow on the plastic wings that cause it to spin in the water and attract fish as I pose the question: "Why would a savvy fish like the king salmon bite such an odd-looking contraption when it looks nothing whatsoever like the food that it has been eating out at sea for the past three to five years?" The obvious answer is that it is fished at about eye level for a fish swimming upstream with "love" on his mind and, out of frustration, it snaps at it to get it out of the way!

The application I make to the group is that our "anger triggers" are much the same. Statements like, "My spouse or my kids really know how to push my buttons" show us that, much like the mighty king salmon, when our family or co-workers happen to "throw out the bait" in our direction (perhaps with an attitude of disrespect or rudeness), we often "take the bait" and snap at them in anger. During those classes, I usually pass out tiny "Spin-n-Glo" lures (minus the hook) for the class members to keep in their pockets as a reminder NOT to take the bait! In unison, several times we repeat, *"Don't take the bait! Don't take the bait!"* As the group continues for several weeks, it is a blessing to hear various members bring "show and tell" stories of how they scored a win by remembering this little tool.

CHAPTER 12

A Fish Out of Water

I t rains a lot in certain parts of Alaska. Ketchikan has an annual rainfall of 162.27 inches. Seward usually gets about 67 inches a year while semi-arid Fairbanks may only get 11 inches. Generally, rainfall around south-central Alaska is more of a steady drizzle than an outright downpour or "gully washer" which other parts of the country experience. Occasionally, though, a rogue weather pattern will hit the state and the results are usually floods. Often, these occur during the summer or early fall months when the salmon are filling the smaller streams to spawn.

Rainy Days

One September the weather currents from the "lower 48" sent the remnant of a tropical storm barreling up to Alaska with the brunt of it making landfall in Seward. It rained hard for several days without let-up, pushing streams over their banks and washing out bridges. Now most folks are not aware of this little tip, but when the rains come and the rivers and creeks are muddy and high in the fall, Seward silver fishing can be incredible. The fish seem to be confused by the raging waters and mill around the shore in schools, unsure of where their river or creek entrances are. The dirty water also fools them into thinking they are submerged in the water when, in reality, their backs and tails can be several inches above the surface. If catching them with a fishing rod weren't so much fun, and it weren't illegal, you could walk along the shore and pick them up by hand.

During the storm I am talking about, one of the creeks on the outskirts of town was flowing over the highway and you could actually watch salmon swim across the road! They were literally fish out of water!

I Know How Those Fish Feel

I discovered, first hand, what it feels like to be the proverbial fish out of water when one of my sojourns out of Alaska found me ministering in the Washington, D. C. area. Believe me, the twelve lanes of traffic careening around the Capital Beltway are a drastic difference from the two-laner in Nikiski, Alaska, where there isn't even one stoplight!!

Part of the ministry I was doing back then involved conducting divorce recovery and other seminars around the United States. Through her make-up artist who attended our church, I was introduced to TV news anchor and movie personality, Doris McMillon, and was subsequently asked to be a guest on her daily live TV show, "On The Line," which aired nationally on the BET Network.

My Guest Today Is . . .

"Five, four, three" . . . the director of the show counted down and then silently flashed two fingers, then one, and then pointed to the talk show host, Doris McMillon. We were on live TV. Each show was aired live one day a week and then replayed via tape the next. With her winning smile and vibrant voice, Doris introduced me as her guest. This was a long, long ways from fishing a lonely stream in Alaska or leading a Bible study for a crowd of twenty.

The Problem

My big problem, though, was that a few days before the scheduled TV appearance, I had succumbed to the oak pollen and cherry blossoms and had a full blown case of either a sinus infection or allergies. My nose and sinuses were clogged, my throat raw, and my ears plugged! My voice had the tone quality of a nasal long-distance operator. While I had prayed for a healing miracle, the day of the TV show came and I was still in miserable shape. However, reassured by the unflappable Doris, the show went on as scheduled.

My Dad Would Croak to See This

Arriving at the studio in 90-degree heat with equal humidity, I was ushered into an air conditioned "make-up" room. "Make-up," I thought. "Don't they know that I was raised on a farm and Coggins men don't *do* make-up?" Well, a few minutes later I left that room wearing rouge and lipstick and some sort of plaster mix that they put on my balding head with the explanation that I may have sweat coming out of my elbows and fingertips, but I would not have any on my forehead! That mask was so thick that I could wiggle my eyebrows and feel the hair on the back of my head move!

From the make-up room, I was whisked away to either the "blue" or "green" room where I was to wait until someone came to escort me to the set where Doris' show would be filmed. This room was one floor up and I could look down from it to the various sets that were being set up for use. In one of them, I recognized the press secretary for the President of the United States as he was preparing for an interview. I had a sudden flashback to my childhood when my nickname was "bashful" because I was so shy and wondered how in the world I wound up here at this moment!

Showtime!

Before I could make an escape, a studio aide tugged at my arm and away we went to the set where Doris was waiting under the lights for me. I think I must have appeared like a jackrabbit caught in the headlights of an oncoming car because Doris laughingly encouraged me to relax and that all would go well. "There will be about 15 million people watching this, and I just know the Lord will help you," were her final remarks before that countdown started and we were on the air. Just like Doris had promised, God came through and gave me good answers to respond to the people who called in with questions from all across the country. That 30-minute slot of ministry was over in what seemed like just a few heartbeats. God had indeed been there for me when I was so far out of my comfort zone that He was the only one who could. As she walked off the set, Doris smiled and called out to me, "See, I told you so."

Since that experience of being a fish out of water, I have been on TV many times. While it still makes me more nervous than I like to be, I know by experience that the Lord can and will be there for me in spite of the intimidating circumstances. The next time you find yourself miles outside of your comfort zone and your faith and courage being put *on the line*, just lean hard on the Lord, your source, who is " . . . The Lord strong and mighty, the Lord mighty in battle" (Psalm 24:8, KJV). He hasn't lost one yet.

CHAPTER 13

Reputations

Long before I ever got to know him personally, I felt like I knew him because of his reputation. Vern Nowell is a wiry sourdough Alaskan known by many as a very skilled woodsman, hunter, trapper, fisherman, Super-Cub bush pilot, sled dog driver, homesteader, well-driller, explosives expert, and, last but not least, truly accomplished story-teller. Walking toward the front door of the church on my first Sunday at North Kenai Chapel, Vern and his wife, Sharon, were the first to approach me and welcome me as their new pastor.

Retired now from some of his more dangerous airborne and dog-mushing avocations, he can still work circles around younger men, and his storytelling skills have only been sharpened by age and practice. A few weeks ago I took Vern to lunch and pried a few more stories out of his archives and sat there spellbound for the better part of two hours listening to stories that made me feel like I was right there with him. The more I get to know him, the more convinced I am that his reputation, though glowing, only portrays a fraction of the true Alaskan and genuine man of God that he is. I'd go into bear country any day with Vern.

Sometimes I wonder if it is the rare air that bush pilots breathe while flying their tiny, but powerful, planes at the top of the world, but a good number of these men are also great tellers of tales. Most have walked away from more than one hair-raising landing or close call. Chuck Gold, my old fishing partner and an incredible bush pilot, plopped us on more than one squeaky short gravel strip near a fish-laden wilderness river and, thankfully, always got us home at the end of the day. He could tell fishing and hunting stories that were so realistic that it would have me swatting imaginary mosquitoes in the dead of winter.

Jimmy Jet was an Oklahoma transplant, respected builder of houses, and a Super Cub pilot to boot. Jimmy could spin a yarn that would make you almost taste and smell the moose tenderloin steaks sizzling in a frying pan at his Stoney River hunting camp, all without exaggerating. Jerry Olson, an artist with a chainsaw or an airplane, could keep you riveted as he humbly told of God directing him to land on a snowy cliff to rescue another downed pilot from certain death.

And Don Shields, though not a pilot at all, can keep you in gut-busting laughter telling the ballad of *Three-Fingered 'Lil*, bagging a one-eyed elk, or recounting the time his brother-in-law called a big bull moose in close and wound up being treed in his long-johns while his rain-soaked Levi's were drying on the bushes! These guys give new meaning to the expression "colorful Alaskans!" Their reputations are well-earned and listening to them is *not* like that old bush pilot expression, *"...like trying to land into a strong headwind with your flaps down."* Being interpreted, this means that they are not just a lot of hot air!

"Can any good thing come out of . . .?"

I was reading recently in the Gospel of John where Nathaniel, upon hearing that his friend, Phillip, had found the Messiah and that He was Jesus of *Nazareth,* replied, "Can any good thing come out of Nazareth?"(1:46, KJV). Evidently, Nazareth had a reputation as being a gritty little town that didn't amount to much, and anyone born and raised there didn't either.

Reputations can really be misleading. For instance, a person may be known all over town as the village flake, but in recent weeks or months that person may have made some changes and in reality is now on a steady path to being a good person. However, when applying for a job or loan, he may find that his reputation has preceded him in a negative way. On the other hand, a person who has played by the rules and been a good citizen for years may have a sterling reputation among the townsfolk. But a few months before he may have weakened and delved into dishonesty or some dark habit that, if discovered, would ruin his name. In this case, his good reputation has preceded him but does not reflect current reality. Reputations, good or bad, can be misleading. I have discovered that this can be true also of churches as well as of communities or people.

North Kenai

North Kenai Chapel, in the little town of Nikiski, is where I am currently serving as a pastor. This little town was developed back in the late 50s with the discovery of oil near Swanson River and gas fields just off-shore in Cook Inlet. Back in those days, it developed a well-earned reputation as a wild and wooly, often lawless piece of Alaska where alcohol and hard living flowed freely. Forty-plus years later, there are still folks who have heard the stories and think twice before driving out "North Road" as it is called.

While there may be a few characters remaining from those old days, what we have discovered in North Kenai and the little town of Nikiski has been quite contrary to those prevailing winds of rumor . . . and especially in our little church. I have found unity among the pastors and churches in Nikiski that is genuine and provides a haven for folks looking for a safe place to grow in their faith. The postmaster greets even newcomers with a smile and seems to know everyone by name, box number and how many kids they have. I wish I could introduce you to the gallery of fine folks that we get to pastor here. To list their names and qualities would be too long for the space I have here, but let me just say this: If I were to be putting together a team of battle-tested, faithful and fruitful people to go with me to start a new church anyplace on this planet, I would hardly need to look beyond North Kenai Chapel.

Mountain View

Well, perhaps I might look for a few folks in Mt. View Baptist Church in Anchorage. Mountain View is another of those places with a rough reputation. Initially, it was a bedroom community for the military personnel stationed at Fort Richardson and Elmendorf. Over the years, though, it degenerated into a drug infested and crime saturated neighborhood where gunshots were heard regularly. Shortly after we began a year of interim pastoring at this small church, the youth pastor said that he felt he had to move his family to a safer neighborhood. A few days before, he had heard a commotion and gunshots out in the street in front of his house. When he looked outside he discovered a bullet-riddled man bleeding to death on his porch. With a growing crop of little ones to care for, I didn't blame him a bit for moving.

What we discovered, however, is that in spite of the dark side of this community's reputation, the inside of that little fellowship of people was populated by the most awesome, loving and committed saints that would make God's first team *anyplace, anytime*. What a special group of God's precious children. I still keep a collage of photos on my office wall made up of the faces of the moms and dads and children who faithfully offer an oasis in the middle of a difficult place. Perhaps people have been looking in the wrong direction to form the reputation with which this neighborhood has been tagged. This neighborhood is being transformed by these and other "salt of the earth" folks who are paying the dues.

Sometimes I wonder just why the Lord has given me the assignments He has. But with Mountain View, I have no doubt. First, I think the Lord knew that I needed a good dose of love and acceptance and these were just the folks to administer it! Second, about a month into our time there, I invited life-long friend and awesome country-gospel singer Judy Rounds, known far and wide as "Country Jude," to come and sing for the church.

Judy did her usual super job and after the service, when Marveen and I invited her to lunch, she asked us if she could bring along a new friend, Joe Cuddy, who had just extended to her a similar invitation. We had a good time dining at Harley's Old Tyme Restaurant, and when we left for home, Joe and Judy were still talking a mile a minute in the parking lot. A few months later I was elated to perform their wedding ceremony. Would God actually send someone to a place just to arrange for two incredible treasures in His kingdom to meet one another? I reckon He can if He wants to and it's fine by me!

Sardis, Alaska?

No, I have not pastored a church in Sardis, Alaska, nor is there even a town here by that name. Sardis is a church mentioned in a letter from Jesus (Revelation 3:1) through the apostle John in which Jesus took them to task by saying that He was aware that they had a reputation as being an alive and "cookin'"(my addition) church, but in reality they were dead. While not exactly words worthy of celebrating with a pot-luck dinner in the fellowship hall, Jesus went on to encourage this fledgling flock to repent, get their priorities right, and when the end comes, He would be proud to welcome them into heaven!

So, that is the *good and bad news* about reputations. While we may cringe knowing that God has a front-row seat to view the reality of what is going on in our lives, He sees our failings through the eyes of mercy and compassion. And, like I saw on the reader board of a great church in Nikiski last week: *God doesn't grade on the curve . . . He grades on the CROSS.* That sure sounds good to me.

CHAPTER 14

God Tracks

I had been in Alaska only a few months and was pastoring a little church in the end-of-the-road community of Homer when I was invited by two old "sourdough" Alaskans to go along with them on their annual moose hunt. What a treat for a Cheechako (rookie) like me to tag along with these seasoned veterans who owned the local drugstore, Howard Myhill and Vern Mutch. I was all eyes, ears and excitement as we made our way into the hunting area at the headwaters of the Anchor River. They rode on a little four-wheel-drive rig that was loaded with our gear. I walked behind, and those eager eyes of mine didn't miss the fact that there were frequent bear tracks along the muddy road. But with these two Alaskan legends as my partners, I was only a little concerned.

The first signs of daylight the following morning found us heading out in three directions along the seismograph trails that crisscrossed the entire area like a checker board. These were small little roads cut in by the USGS (United States Geological Survey) in order for them to install seismographs to measure earthquake activity, which, by the way, is a very common occurrence in Alaska. The trails were roughly one mile square. Our plan was for each of us to slowly walk our four-mile route looking for moose and meet back at the camp later that day.

I was "on my own" in the Alaska wild for the first time! Gulp! It took several hours to complete the circuit, and I found myself back at the beginning point to discover that the other two were still out in the woods. Figuring I had walked too fast, I decided to make another quick trip down the trail.

After a few hundred yards of following my own tracks down the trail, I suddenly noticed that my tracks were now not the only ones on the trail. Along with my boot tracks were some HUGE bear tracks, ON TOP OF MINE. It dawned on me with a jolt of fear that there was a very large brown bear who was tracking ME! My two guides had given me a little wilderness instruction earlier that you can generally tell the size of a bear by putting your foot sideways in his track. Trying this method, I discovered that my size 11 boot fit nicely into his track with a little room to spare. Yikes! My already active adrenal glands hit overdrive!!

So, with a bullet in the chamber of my new 30.06 rifle, I began to inch my way ahead while my eyes were scanning in all directions like a swivel-headed owl! I had walked no more than twenty yards when, without knowing they were there, I almost stepped on a couple of spruce hens which exploded into the air right in front of me. I am not sure who was more startled, them or me. However, I think I will claim the honor since I had to sit down on a log and rest because my legs were so weak from the experience that I couldn't walk.

Later that night, while sitting around the campfire retelling our day's adventures, Howard and Vern laughed until their sides hurt at my rookie day in the wilderness. I never did spot that big bear, but you can bet your bottom dollar I KNOW what a bear track looks like, and I also learned another way to know you are in big bear country.

Thanks to my patient mentors, they told me that if I were hiking in the woods and came upon a spruce tree that had bear hair clinging to the bark, I should look up and see if the bear had signed in by biting a big chunk out of the tree as high as he could reach by standing on his hind legs. This is one way the bears "mark their territory," and any intruder, bear or human, had better take notice. In some parts of Alaska it is not unusual to see trees with this tell-tale "bite" that is ten to twelve feet above the ground.

God Tracks

Now, let's talk about God tracks . . . those ways you can determine that your circumstances are marked by *His* presence and plan. I believe that as surely as the trained eye can spot bear, moose, elk or squirrel tracks in the snow, we can also learn to recognize God's tracks in our lives. You just have to know what to look for and that sometimes takes awhile to learn. For me . . . a lifetime.

Back in the sixties, when I was attending Bible college, the school had mandatory chapel attendance for all students, everyday, all year long. Occasionally the call of the local doughnut shop would beckon and my roommate and I might skip chapel, but not on Fridays. You see, Friday was when there was usually a guest speaker who might be a local pastor or guest speaker visiting the northwest. The reason those Friday chapel services were so well attended was that, odds were, the speaker would focus on the hottest topic for any aspiring pastor, minister or young person: *"How to know God's will for your life!"* The sixties was an action era, and above all else we wanted to figure out what God wanted us to do and get with the program and do it! Having your life matter in the big picture was, and still is, the pearl of great price.

Groucho's Rubber Duckie

So, with baited breath, we'd listen Friday after Friday to various takes on that subject. Looking back, it reminded me of the old Groucho Marx TV show when a guest on the program would say the "magic word" and a little rubber duck would be lowered into the set with a cash prize for the lucky winner. We kept hoping that someday, sometime, one of those speakers would say just the right words and suddenly the plan and will of God for our lives would burst into focus. Then, at last, we'd know. But, frankly, the duck never came down and there remained a gnawing sense of urgency to "know" God's will as the years went by.

God Does Guide Us

Years later, looking back on those early days of striving and straining to "hear from God" on some decision or direction in life seemed pretty immature and desperate. In some ways now, while it isn't quite as difficult to recognize God's activity around me, realizing that the end of the runway of life is not all that far away makes the stakes seem higher and the desire to be in the "sweet spot" of God's will even more intense.

Several guidelines have shown that it is possible to make God's best choices for your life, your own. First, there is a wonderful little book by Bob Mumford entitled *Take Another Look at Guidance* (Logos International, 1971). He says that in discerning if a planned direction is from God, three things, like beacon lights, will line up to guide you into the harbor: God's

Word, the peace of God, and circumstances. If one ingredient is missing, just wait. God will never violate His Word by leading you to do something sinful, nor will He violate your own conscience (peace), or leave the particulars of your new direction without an apparent first step for you to take (circumstances).

God is a creative God by nature, and He has unlimited ways with which He can communicate with us, not the least of which is *His peace*. Colossians 3:16 (Amplified Bible) says that the peace of Christ will act as an umpire in our lives, helping us decide "with finality all questions that arise in your minds." It is pretty simple. If there is no peace, hold steady on course until there is.

There are many of kinds of animal tracks in the woods, and you can learn what track is made by which animal. You can even tell by close examination if a moose or elk track is made by a bull or a cow. Likewise, when you are a follower of Jesus and you trust Him to guide your decisions, His tracks and His voice are unmistakable. He wasn't kidding around when He said in John 10:27, "My sheep hear my voice, and I know them, and they follow me."

CHAPTER 15

Old Hands

It had been years since I had fished one of those "midnight" openings for king salmon on the Anchor River. A couple of decades ago I finally realized that, while those all-night fishing marathons are fun and generally produce fish in the smokehouse, it takes much longer now to recoup from a lost night of sleep than it did when I was a younger man. But now and then, even old fishermen succumb to the adrenaline rush that comes with standing on the riverbank, counting the remaining minutes before you and countless other equally anxious fishermen can start fishing at the stroke of midnight. This scene has repeated itself for generations since the Alaska Fish and Game Department opted to make the king salmon season on certain streams on the Kenai Peninsula a weekend only fishery that opens Friday night at midnight for the duration of the king run in late May through June.

King Salmon Fever

My wife, Marveen, who is always game for such adventure,

was visiting family in Colorado, so I was fishing this night with a long-time fishing buddy, Hilmer Kiser, his wife Maranna, and their 8-year-old grandson, Tony. We arrived at the Anchor River in time to rig up our lines and walk a few sections of the river to pick a good spot. At around 11:30 p.m. we were in *our spot* at the old "Slide Hole" along with about twenty other fishermen. Downstream from me was Tony, who was literally trembling with excitement to start fishing. For an 8-year-old the minutes dragged by. I jokingly said that maybe the time would go faster if he just curled up on my coat and took a nap. His reply mentioned something about my unstable mental condition to suggest such a thing!

The Old Fisherman

Upstream from me a few feet was an old gentleman sitting on a log, just staring into the river. I greeted him and wished him luck catching a big king. When he smiled a return greeting I thought, "I remember this man!" So, I walked over and asked if his name was what I thought it was. Yes, he was the man I had remembered fishing on this same river nearly 35 years ago. He and his brother were fixtures on the Anchor River every year and were known as courteous and skilled fishermen who almost always got their limit of fish before most of the rest of us.

For the next 30 minutes we sat on his log talking about the old timers we both knew, how fishing had changed, and how sad he was because his brother wasn't alive any longer to enjoy these moments with him. He pointed out four of his grandsons who were lined up on the opposite shore in prime fishing spots. He allowed that he would be over on the other side of the river with them, but his legs just weren't stable enough for him to wade across the river with its swift current and slippery rocks. He apologized for having such a soft voice but explained that Parkinson's disease had taken a toll on him in recent years. He also admitted that his hands weren't very agile anymore and he might be a little slow retrieving his line. Between minute by minute inquiries by young Tony about "how much time was left," this old gentleman and I savored what may be one of his last midnight openings.

It was then that I noticed his hands. In his 80s, his hands told the story of a life lived as a pioneer in Alaska's last frontier. Old wounds had healed but left their nicks and scars on his battered hands. A few fingers, bent in awkward directions, bespoke a few broken bones in years gone by. As the glow from the sunset in the west began to fade, and only seconds remained before the fishing frenzy would begin, his old hands reached into his bait can and retrieved a big glob of salmon eggs which he attached slowly to his hook. There was no wasted motion as he baited his hook.

"Well, it's time to get down to business," he quipped as he stood, stripped ten yards of line off his reel and tossed his bait into the river along with the rest of the fishermen. Within seconds, his grandsons across the river were fighting kings as were two or three guys on our side. Young Tony was a picture of 100% concentration as he cast his line time after time in hopes of being one of the lucky ones. Numerous times the old gentleman and I had to pull our lines out of the water to allow others room to play their fish. Even young Tony had a big fish on for several minutes before it broke off and temporarily broke his heart.

After about an hour of watching real life dramas of "the thrill of victory and the agony of defeat" being played out all around us, the old fisherman and I sat down on our log to assess why neither of us had even a bite. "Must be 'snake-bit' tonight," he mused as he mustered up the energy to re-bait his hook and stand up one more time to cast into the dark water. "Can't catch nothing unless your line's in the water," he muttered. It was nearly dark but this old fish warrior just kept fishing with the eternal hope of youth in every cast. Just one more cast! But I noticed that he was getting slower and slower in his fishing motion. About then one of his grandsons waded across the river dragging a nice fish he'd caught. After nodding his approval, the old fisherman decided he was getting weary and would call it a night and head for home. "See you next time. Nice talking with you," he said as he gathered up his gear, gave the river one last lingering glance, and headed down the path. I followed him a few minutes later.

By six that morning I was finally home, and I groaned as I laid my sore body in bed, exhausted. But, surprisingly, sleep didn't come as easily as I had expected it would. I couldn't get the mental picture of that old pioneer fisherman's hands to stop replaying in the theatre of my mind. Then I made the connection.

Another Set of Old Hands

I reached over to a shelf by the side of the bed, pulled out a picture album, and by the light of the morning sun now streaming into the bedroom, I fumbled through the pages until I found it. It was a photo of my dad's left hand and my mother's left hand that had been taken at their fiftieth wedding anniversary a few months before my father passed away. Though they had different nicks, scars and age spots, they had a similar history written in them as did those of my midnight fishing friend. Then my mind wandered to the day that my mom, along with us four children, made a sad trip to the funeral home to see my father in the casket that now held his body.

I remember it like it was yesterday. My mom was the first to approach the casket as we stood beside her. My dad's body lay there, hands folded over his chest, eyes closed and, after a lifetime of hard work to provide for his family, a year or so of debilitating cancer, and a stroke, his weary body was at rest. I will always remember his hands ... weather-worn and strong. Then, in an act that told the story of a life of love and fulfillment with her husband, as she did in life, she tenderly framed his face with her hands and looked beyond those closed eyelids and into the eyes of the love of her life. His hands, her hands, in life and in death, were amazing instruments of love.

The Nail-Pierced Hands

Someday, when the last fish has been caught and the last midnight opening on the Anchor River has come and gone, if we have made our peace with God, we will be able to personally see the nail-pierced hands of Jesus. Those hands of the carpenter from Nazareth that held him to the cross as the Messiah will be the hands that welcome us into eternity. Those hands, calloused from years spent working with tools, were the ones that reached out to grasp the equally calloused hands of a Jewish fisherman named Peter, who had begun to sink in the stormy water. It will be those same hands that you will recognize—as the hands that rescued *you*.

CHAPTER 16

The Arctic Diet

I love living in Alaska. The mountains, ocean, abundant space and awesome fishing are hard to resist. I read someplace that if you ever visit Alaska, you never really leave, and I guess I am a case in point. Since arriving in Alaska as a wide-eyed young man on Thanksgiving Day, 1971, I have left a few times: twice to fulfill a church planting vision and ministry in the Washington, D. C. area; once to be a part of my wife's dream to live a full year at her family's cabin in the Rockies. And once more to test my own ability to open a counseling practice in Steamboat Springs, Colorado.

But here we are, back in Alaska. It seems like every few years I hit a restless streak and feel a need to try something new. Perhaps I was bitten by what Robert Service describes in his poem, "The Men Who Don't Fit In," where he says, " . . . If they ever went straight, they might go far . . . " referring to that urge to wander and explore new territory (*The Spell of the Yukon,* Barse and Hopkins Publishers, 1907).

Recreational Eating

There is one aspect of Alaskan life, however, that has given me more difficulty than the gypsy urges, and that is what I have come to call "recreational eating!" Now I know that eating or overeating is certainly not unique to the north, but the fact that Alaskans consume more ice cream per capita than any other state might give you a clue. Perhaps it is those dark winter nights that spur on the desire to celebrate everything with food with one thinking that, "Come summer I'll be fishing, hiking, and hunting and work off this winter blubber!"

A trip to Anchorage most times ignites an internal guidance lock on places known to all, like the BBQ Pit, Lucky Wishbone, Arctic Roadrunner and Gwennie's Old Alaskan Restaurant! Most of these places are decorated with Alaskana such as mounted fish, bears, moose, and pictures of customers that have been faithful diners for generations. I have had phone calls from misplaced Alaskans from the far flung reaches of the country requesting that if I come to visit, could I please bring some favorite sauce or a souvenir menu from one of their old haunts?

I think it was somewhere around age thirty that I noticed my waist size began getting bigger while my pant length remained the same. As a result, I have tried a number of ways to alter the shape of my body to look and feel more fit and trim instead of like a *wanna-be* sumo wrestler!

The Buddy System

One year a good friend and attorney in Anchorage confided that he thought it would help us both if we adopted the buddy system that would require a daily list to be kept of everything that went into our mouths and a nightly call to each other to report our progress. It worked pretty well for awhile until I made the mistake of mentioning it in one of my sermons on how we need to encourage one another in the church. What that did was enlist roughly 1500 volunteer cheerleaders who doubled as spies and witnesses to any infractions. They even put a picture of a blimp-sized body in the church bulletin (with my face on it), and listed my weekly progress down the bathroom scales. This is where I learned a valuable lesson that accountability is not the only ingredient to success.

Eventually, my dieting buddy and I started avoiding each other, and the day someone chastised me at the counter of a nearby 7-Eleven store while I held a Hostess Cupcake and Dr. Pepper in my clutches signaled the end of that public dieting adventure. Occasionally, thirty years later, I have had folks remind me of how much fun that was—*for them.*

A few years later, after being subjected to clandestine copies of some sort of high fiber diet being left where I was sure to see them, I decided to venture out into the Alaskan wilderness on a moose hunting trip with my old friend, Ben Pollen. I only took health food, nuts, granola, and other food items to eat that were only slightly tastier than their wrapper. His father-in-law, famed bush pilot Cleo McMahan, flew us out into the wilderness and dropped us off miles from the nearest road. Ben, a guy with seemingly no weight issues, had the usual basic food groups represented in his grub sack— things like weenies, chips, cookies, and soda. On our first night, I was starting to experience sugar withdrawals and had a nasty headache while he sat there and cooked his hot dogs, oblivious to my misery. By the second night, I was starting to get cranky and by the third night I was considering offering a trade of my hunting rifle for just one of his hot dogs!

My big mistake was discovering that Alaska's abundant

blueberries do have a fairly high sugar content, and they were everywhere. So, while we were hiking around hunting, I ate handful after handful of these tasty sweet little berries not realizing that all of those berry skins were having a cleansing effect on my digestive system that would indeed prove a very quick way to lose weight. Late that night, a storm blew into our area bringing with it freezing rain and high winds. It was cold and damp, and happiness was being snuggled into a goose-down sleeping bag with no need to get out until dawn. That was when the abdominal rumbles started to bring enough discomfort that I had to make no less than a half-dozen trips in my long-johns and boots out into that dark, chilling rain to take care of urgent business.

By dawn of the fourth day, the nearest thing to paradise was the sound of that little Super Cub landing on that remote lake to pick up us fearless hunters for the ride back to civilization. With no moose to ferry out, and me about ten pounds lighter, the take-off was a piece of cake! As soon as we landed and loaded our gear in my truck, we headed for Gakona, the nearest town, where I pulled in to get gas and a fistful of candy bars, a bag of chips and a Dr. Pepper. Arctic diet #2 was officially logged in history as too much pain for the gain (or loss)!

Current Events

The other day, after stepping on those lyin' curr' dog bathroom scales that taunt me every morning, we decided to spend some of our tax refund on a treadmill and a bicycle. Now, the bike riding is a fun activity in the summer but, to date, the only sweat that treadmill has created has been that which we generated getting that miserably heavy thing up the stairs to the room with a view of the woods in our backyard. But hope springs eternal and tomorrow is another opportunity to invest in a longer, healthier life.

I finally gave up the search to find a rogue Bible commentary which says that "Godliness with contentment is great gain" actually refers to a spiritual pursuit to go through the pot luck line three times to work on that "great gain" part!!

Chapter 17

Terminal Gear

Fishing on Alaska's Kenai River for trophy king salmon is an experience like no other. With the record sport-caught king salmon being 97 lbs. 4 oz., and reports of kings over 100 lbs. being taken at sea in nets, it makes your heart beat faster and your breath come a little shorter when you have a line in the same water where it is possible that a descendant of those record kings just might be under your boat at that moment. As you are drifting along, you're hoping that every bump or tug on your line, be it a snag, a rock, or a smaller fish, just may be the one! This is not the kind of fishing you do while taking a nap with the line tied to your toe or using an ultra-light fly rod with 4 lb. test leader tied to a fake gnat or mosquito. This is mortal combat with heavy gear and human muscle pitted against fish muscle and the strong current of the mighty Kenai River.

Alaska's Famed Kenai River

Fishing on the Kenai River also has its own jargon. One

doesn't get a "nibble or bite" when fishing for kings. Using 30-40 lb. test line and a 50 lb. test leader, a bite is called a "take down" and a fish on is called a "hook up!" When a take down and hook up occurs, all other lines onboard are quickly reeled in and a member of the fishing party extends the handle on the landing net and stands it upright so all other boats in the vicinity can see that you are fighting a fish and can maneuver out of your way to give you optimum opportunity to land the fish. Then, the chase is on, often taking the boat and fishermen several miles down the river in pursuit of the big fish that literally "tears" downstream in an attempt to free itself.

I should add, too, that setting the hook on a big king salmon doesn't just require a little tug on the rod. A savvy fisherman will jerk backwards with all his might two or three times to make sure the hook is driven deep into the jaw of old Mr. King Salmon. Often a boat captain or guide can be heard up and down the river excitedly shouting instructions like, "hit it . . . hit it again . . . set the hook . . . hit it harder!!"

The Big One

The above scenario happened to me a few years ago. About mid-morning, while drifting along, bait bouncing on the bottom, suddenly the reel began to sing and the rod bent down to the water as a fish took it. It was a serious "take down." A few hard jerks back and we had a "hook up" and the battle was on! At first, it didn't feel like it was an especially big fish. Then it tore across the river and peeled off around a hundred yards of line with no effort at all.

The boat driver, my long time friend and pastor from Seward, Hilmer Kiser, with lots of experience on the river, turned the boat downstream and gave chase in an attempt to catch up before all the line was gone. Reeling like mad, my arms ached and my heart and adrenaline were pumping. Then we saw him roll—a swirl of red-tinged silver broke the water and I saw its huge tail slap the surface as he dove for the bottom and headed downstream again. When we caught up with him, he just seemed to sulk, not moving and holding just below the surface so we couldn't quite see him. Unexpectedly, he came up to within a few inches of the surface and turned sideways drifting for a moment right beside the boat. Hilmer, seizing the opportunity, grabbed the net and with skill learned only after years of experience, slipped it under the fish and scooped him up beside the boat. He called for help and one of the other guys on the boat grabbed the net with him and they hauled him over the side and right into my lap!

As we all stood there staring at this beautiful and very large fish on the bottom of the boat, the lone remaining hook (we used a two hook set-up, which was legal then) just fell out of his mouth. As it turned out, this really was a miracle fish. He weighed 70-1/2 lbs., and upon close examination, the Gamagatsu trailer hook (considered by many the best you can buy) had broken off, and the one hook that held him was bent almost straight. One more flip of his tail and dive to the bottom and he would have been gone. It turned out that my fish was one of the largest landed on the river that day. It was funny though, as word of it spread up and down the river among the fishermen, it grew up to 72 pounds and by the end of the day it was 78 pounds. Amazing!

The Importance of Terminal Gear

The title of this true life tale is Terminal Gear for a reason. Terminal gear is what is at the end of your fishing line where the hooks, sinker, swivels and lures, etc., are all tied together in such a way that they will enable you to present the bait just off the bottom of the river where the big fish swim. You can have the best boat and motor, the best rod and reel, and even the best line that money can buy, but if your knots aren't tied right, the hooks aren't sharp or the line is frayed even a little, your terminal gear will fail and the fish will be just one more story about the one that got away. Regular checks of your "terminal gear" are essential for success on the river.

I think the same is true with our lives—our relationships with God and others. We just can't take for granted those *knots*, those relational connections that are so vital to a successful marriage or for a genuinely close relationship with the Lord. Jesus instructed us to "abide in the vine." The Amplified Bible translates that as "abide vitally united to Me [the Lord]" (John 15:7). I encourage you to check the vital connections in your life. Are you living your priorities and values? Are you really connected to your wife, children and friends in a healthy way, or are you taking those knots for granted? Are you really walking hand in hand and heart to heart with the Lord or are you on "cruise control" and just a little out of touch?

Remember, when you suddenly get a "take down" or "hook up" with some of life's trophy problems and challenges, there isn't time to reel up and check to be sure your knots are secure and your hooks are in good shape. You are locked into a battle, and if you are to succeed your terminal gear had better hold.

CHAPTER 18

Miracle Moose

Each spring in Alaska an amazing miracle takes place. Moose cows find themselves a quiet thicket of trees and give birth to another year's crop of calves. Now, you may be wondering why I refer to that natural process as being a miracle, but have you ever noticed that an adult moose isn't exactly what you would call beautiful or handsome? First, they are mostly legs! A mature moose can stand seven feet tall and weigh up to 1500 pounds! Second, their most noteworthy feature is their huge, bulbous schnozzola (nose) that sort of droops down with an expression that perhaps only another moose might find attractive. This appendage is functional, allowing a moose to actually eat under water if need be. Functional? Yes. Beautiful? Hardly!

The Miracle

The miracle I am referring to is the incredibly cute little rust-colored babies they have. How can anything that homely make babies that cute? It must be a miracle! They are adorable and we have spent many hours watching them cavort around on their wobbly legs while learning the ropes of wilderness survival from their patient and very protective mothers. Some folks contend that a cow moose defending her young can be more dangerous than a grizzly bear. I am not sure about that but I have seen them put their ears back and charge people or other critters, lashing out furiously with their sharp front hooves. Occasionally, the news will report that someone has been trampled to death by an angry or cornered moose.

In my own unscientific analysis, I think I have figured out why they are so fiercely protective of their young. It is not unusual for a cow moose to have twin calves, and occasionally even triplets. Can you imagine what a mother moose goes through being pregnant and having anywhere from four to twelve sharp little moose hooves kicking and squirming in her already crowded abdomen? It is difficult enough for moose to survive the rigors of an Arctic winter but even more challenging to find enough food to feed the whole crew inside her. So, after going through all of that plus the trauma of giving birth all by herself, it is no wonder she gets a little cranky and upset if anything or anybody threatens her hard-earned family unit.

Moose can be dangerous in other ways as well. According to the Moose Federation's website, there were over 1,300 moose/vehicle collisions in 2003 resulting in $18,000,000 dollars in property damage. When a car and a moose collide, both usually receive some degree of damage.

"I Hit a Mooses!"

One winter night while driving back to Anchorage from Seward, a sleek, black, sporty, Camaro shot past me going much too fast for the slippery conditions. A few miles down the road, I pulled up behind this same vehicle which was sitting crossways in the road with a crumpled hood, smashed windshield and squashed roof. Thankfully, all five passengers were uninjured, but the moose lying dead beside the roadway didn't fare so well. One of the accident victims approached me and in broken English asked if I could call the police because, "I hit a mooses!" He was so shook up I think he thought he'd run into a whole herd of them. It turned out that the car contained five Portuguese fishermen who had gotten shore leave in Seward, borrowed a car and were on their way to Anchorage to see the sights when their low-slung vehicle ran right under a moose which was standing broadside on the highway.

While I have never collided with a moose personally, I have had some very close calls. In mid-winter, when the snow is deep, moose tend to hang out around highways and railroads making for easier walking. Once, while driving a small Volkswagen on a mountain road near Homer, I rounded a corner to find a huge bull moose in my lane, fortunately going my direction at full gallop. I downshifted and applied the brakes as fast as I could without going into a slide. But I suddenly found myself up close and personal with this moose's huge rear end as my front bumper nudged his hind Achilles tendons. By interrupting his stride, his feet got tangled, and I thought for a second that I was going to have a 1500 pound moose sitting on the flimsy hood of my car!

Thankfully, however, he recovered his balance and leapt into the deep snow piled along the road. After a few lunges, he found stable footing, stopped and glared at me with flared nostrils and a very annoyed expression. I drove on numbly grateful that I hadn't wound up with an angry Bullwinkle in my lap!

Moose Nugget Earrings?

If you wish, you can go online and find photo galleries of

moose in all kinds of poses. Some show urban moose with Christmas lights dangling from their antlers, while others are seen cooling off during the summer in backyard swimming pools. For chocolate lovers, some shops carry wood carvings of a bull moose especially equipped so when you lift its tail, it will dispense candy from the north end of a southbound critter. How cute. Some entrepreneurial folks go out into the woods and collect moose droppings which they bake, varnish or paint and turn them into earrings or other designer jewelry for the discriminating shopper. And, there is a terrific little bakery in Soldotna, Alaska, called "The Moose Is Loose," where you can get moose-shaped cookies or visit their gift shop and buy red boxer shorts with moose stenciled on them. Alaska is indeed a "moosey" place!

Moose Burglars

One summer our phone rang at around 3 a.m., bringing me out of a deep sleep with a start. A pastor's phone rarely rings at that hour with good news. It was one of the gals from our church sounding anxious about something, but with my hearing aids in their container on my nightstand, I had difficulty understanding her. What I thought I heard her say was that she had shot her husband and she was wondering if I could bring my truck over and help her remove his carcass! With this little tidbit of misinformation, I asked her to please hold on while I put in my hearing aid! This sounded serious and I needed to get the story straight.

What actually happened is this. She and her family weren't exactly flush with cash that spring, so they had planted a large garden in their backyard to help feed their three growing boys. However, when the plants were about six inches high, a foraging cow moose had helped herself and had mowed them down to little nubbins, forcing them to replant almost the whole garden. This time, they put up a twine fence around the garden area and armed it with a tin-can alarm system in case another moose came calling. At about ten on the evening of her call, that is just what occurred. When the cans started rattling, both she and her husband ran outside shouting and the moose beat a hasty retreat.

Then, again at about midnight, it came back and the scene was repeated. Sometime around two in the morning, this persistent garden raider returned for some free salad. This time, however, her husband said he was too sleepy to fool with any more moose and informed her that if she wanted to go out and do guard duty, she could just go right ahead.

Alaska Annie

With anger and some fear, she grabbed his .45 caliber handgun and ran shouting out into the backyard in her bathrobe. By the time she got there, the marauding moose was in the middle of the garden and had a mouthful of those tender young vegetable plants. It refused to move when she got closer and yelled even louder. Suddenly, her presence made the moose angry and it lowered its ears and came charging at her, full-speed ahead. In self-defense, she raised the .45, took quick aim and put a bullet right between the charging moose's eyes, stopping it dead in its tracks, crushing lettuce, cabbage and broccoli as it fell.

Her call to me was not to see if I could help her dispose of a dead husband, but to see if I could help her move the dead moose's carcass out of the garden to a spot where they could skin it and salvage the meat. Now, it would seem that after all they'd been through, this family would have been entitled to fill their freezer with moose meat, but I knew the law saw it differently. It is illegal to shoot a moose just to defend property such as a garden, so I advised her to calm down and call the State Troopers to come and investigate before they did anything to the moose. She reluctantly called the police who came promptly to check out her story and proceeded to call a group of accidental moose-kill volunteers who came, butchered the animal, and gave the meat to a local homeless shelter.

They didn't get to enjoy one moose burger for all their trouble. The good news, however, is that our friend was not charged with illegally discharging a weapon within city limits. And because her deadly "between the eyes" shot indicated that indeed the moose was charging her, she was cleared on that count as well. Since then I have given her the unofficial nickname of *Alaska Annie* (after wild-west sharp-shooter Annie Oakley) and have informed her that if any bad guys ever decide to invade Alaska, I want her on my team! This gal can shoot!

In Ecclesiastes chapter three, the Bible says that there is a purpose for everything under the sun that God created. I assume that includes the uniquely adapted and expansive nose of the Alaska moose that enables it to survive in one of the world's harshest environments. However, I am glad that when the Lord was handing out body parts for Alaskans like me, He didn't give me one of those!

CHAPTER 19

R-e-l-a-x

Jerry Olson is one of Alaska's famed bush pilots who is more "at home" in the seat of his Piper Super Cub on floats than most of us are in our comfy recliners with the TV remote control at our fingertips. Knowing his reputation as a savvy and skilled pilot, I never hesitated a second when he would ask me if I wanted to make an hour flight to his home near Alexander Lake to fish or hunt. He could maneuver, land, and take off so smoothly that the trips were always enjoyable...well, for the most part.

Relax?

I was in the back seat of his trusty Super Cub when I noticed a small sign taped to one of the interior support beams of the little plane. It was made with one of those little label makers and it said, "Relax!" I was just absorbing the message of the sign when Jerry asked me if I ever got airsick. "Never have," I replied. So, with an encouragement to hang on, he pointed the nose of the plane right down at the ground!

Whooee! What a rush as we went into a power dive!

Then he pulled back on the steering yoke and we gradually leveled out and began an almost vertical climb toward the sun! I could feel the blood in my body arguing with my brain that I should make up my mind whether we were going up or down! I had a momentary flutter in my stomach but kept my breakfast where it belonged. I had that feeling you get when an elevator reaches its destination, sort of like being suspended in zero gravity for a split second. Only this was that feeling times ten as we leveled off. I suggested we might pass on another such flight maneuver as we headed on to our destination. His laughter still rings in my ears. I think this is what big boys do with their toys.

The Five Year Rule

I noticed with my kids that there was about a five year gap between some of their actual escapades and when they decided, in a moment of family joking around, to tell dad what really happened on some occasion. I think it had to do with a *guestimate* that enough time had lapsed so I'd just laugh with them instead of getting angry or meting out some discipline.

I am familiar with this dynamic because I think it is the same one I have applied in keeping my mom informed about some of our adventures in the wilds of Alaska over the years. Understanding that a part of a mom's job description is to alternate between worry and prayer, I didn't want her to lean too heavily into the worry department. So, sometimes a little time lapse is warranted before the *rest of the story* comes to light. Here is the rest of one story.

Kodiak Island Adventure

Kodiak Island has some of the wildest weather in Alaska.

Sitting exposed to the Gulf of Alaska and Aleutian weather patterns, it is not uncommon for the rain to be coming down sideways in the high winds. Landing an aircraft at the Kodiak airport can put new meaning to the phrase, "white-knuckle landing." I remember my first flight into Kodiak aboard a commercial Boeing 737. I noticed that even though we were coming in over the water, there was a *mountain* at the end of the runway. Gulp!

Added to the drama, however, was the fact that the wind was howling and the plane was alternating between sudden drops downward and a sideways motion like someone swishing water around in a gold pan! I realized that the crosswinds at the airport were making this somewhat of a challenge for the pilot, so I opted, with most of the rest of the passengers, to pray like crazy for him and for us. In order to get the plane down, he seemed to be quartering into the wind and just as we were about to touch down, he leveled the plane and we landed, first on one wheel, and then finally both hit the pavement. With a collective sigh of relief we all cheered and clapped his God-assisted performance.

An Alaskan Honorarium

I was in Kodiak for three days before the monsoon rain and wind subsided and they finally reopened the airport. I also remember the pastor of the church where I had preached told me that the church was a little short on funds for an honorarium and he wondered if he could pay me with three five-pound bricks of king crab legs (all shelled out and neatly frozen). I thought about it—for about two seconds—and agreed. His suggestion that I could invite a bunch of good friends over to our home in Anchorage for a crab feast was entertained for another two seconds before laughingly I said,

"You must be kidding! I don't have any friends that good."
The ride home was, thankfully, smooth and uneventful.

Prudhoe Bay

Another assignment we always enjoyed was an invitation
to fly up north to Prudhoe Bay to conduct Christmas or Easter
services. Our friend, Harry Crippen, at the time a fireman in
the Prudhoe Bay oil fields and one of the leaders of the little
non-denominational church made up of workers in that far
north oil operation, set it all up.

Located on the shores of the Beaufort Sea (about as far
north as you can get), the church met in the theatre in the
PBOC (Prudhoe Bay Operations Center) where we were also
provided with overnight sleeping accommodations and delicious meals. Our flight and other expenses were being paid for
by one of the oil companies in a gesture of understanding of
the loneliness that can creep in when employees are away from
their families during these holiday times. We always enjoyed
our trips there and always felt appreciated by the men and
women who work in this very frigid part of the world. I
remember my wife looking earnestly out a tiny window into
the 24-hour winter darkness in hopes of seeing a polar bear,
but one never paid a visit coinciding with ours during the four
or five years we did this.

A Dream Come True

One Prudhoe Bay experience that sticks in my mind
occurred during the early years of the development of this
important oil resource. A friend in our church was a pilot of
a small jet (similar to a Lear Jet, only a little larger), used pri-
marily for flying oil company executives between Anchorage,
Fairbanks and the oil fields. After repeated attempts to

arrange for me to fly along just to see what it was like that far north, he called one day saying that if I could get to the airport in an hour, it was a "go."

I had always had a desire to fly in one of the Air Force's F-4 or F-5 fighters that operated from Elmendorf, AFB in Anchorage, but even a friend who was one of the commanders there couldn't pull enough strings to make it happen. I figured it would never happen. But flying in this hot corporate jet was close enough for me. And up we went. What a thrill!

Zero Visibility

What I hadn't counted on, however, was that when we landed in Prudhoe Bay, the weather kicked up and they had to pull the plane into a hangar and wait until there was at least a quarter-mile visibility where we were or in nearby Pt. Barrow so we could safely take off and have a place to land if there were any problem. After a dinner of steak and shrimp and all the ice cream I could eat, I crashed in an unoccupied bunk until about five in the morning when the pilot awakened me with a start saying that we had to run for the hangar because we had a window of visibility to take off.

For the return trip, I had the privilege of sitting on a retractable jump-seat in the cockpit between the two pilots. I also had on a pair of headphones so I could hear what they were hearing from the control tower. What caused me some trepidation, however, was that I could also see exactly what the pilots could see out the windshield. What I saw wasn't a long string of blue runway lights trailing off into the distance, but two specks of light about fifty feet ahead on either side of the runway. The rest was a blur of blowing snow.

The pilot didn't have to tell me twice to buckle down my seatbelt! It was *securely fastened,* as they say these days. "Hang on," the pilot said, "we are going to make a pretty steep ascent." How right he was! He put the throttles to the firewall and we shot down that runway like a bullet and then, literally, almost straight up! Whew! I could feel the force of the jet engine thrust pushing me back into the seat. Within maybe five seconds at most, we were up out of the blowing ground snow and into the darkness lit only by the galaxies of stars that suddenly appeared. We were on our way home.

Shortly after we reached our cruising altitude at around thirty thousand feet, we leveled off and the pilot pressed some buttons and flipped some switches to put the plane into autopilot mode for the rest of the journey to Anchorage. We had a great time flying into the glowing dawn while he talked about his life and his job. I was living a dream to fly in a speedy little jet when all of a sudden my attention snapped immediately to two flashing amber lights on the control panel accompanied by a shrill beep-beep-beeping sound that told me that something was definitely haywire. Calmly, the pilot pushed a few buttons and informed me that if the plane went above or below the prescribed altitude by several hundred feet, this alarm went off to let them know.

Just before beginning our descent into Anchorage, I heard Anchorage tower control inform our pilot that we were in traffic and that a Japan Airlines 747 was in our "ten o'clock" field of vision. I looked out the left window and sure enough, there it was. The tower instructed the 747 to begin its descent, and it seemed to just fall out of the sky. We also were advised as we followed the 747 into the landing pattern to watch out for jet-wash, the turbulence made by such huge engines.

We landed safely and I thanked my pilot friend for the thrill of a lifetime. Later that day, as I sat in my office at the church, I closed the door, imagined I was sitting in the cockpit

of my own jet, and, strapped into my office chair by an imaginary seatbelt, I blasted off into the Alaskan skies for a re-run
of that adventure.   The live flight was a lot more fun.

Dear Mom
   When my mom reads this story, she will likely agree that
it was a good thing she was at home praying for her son, way
up there in the north. She didn't know what was going on so
she skipped the worrying stage, and just kept a' praying.
Thanks, Mom.

CHAPTER 20

Fishing with the Bears— in the Dark

Fishing in the dark in Alaska can be a memorable experience. While Alaska is renowned for its "midnight sun" in
the summer, there are several months on either side of
that time of year when the sun does go down and it can get
dark, dark, dark for several hours.

It was one of those "dark" times in early summer when my
friend, Marshall, and I decided to hike several miles along the
railroad tracks (now illegal) to a secret spot we had heard of
where a little clear-water creek dumped into a muddy glacier-
fed larger stream just south of Anchorage. We had heard that
the sockeye salmon congregated in that little pocket where the
clear and gray waters mixed and were so thick you could walk
across the stream on their backs (don't believe such tales!).
Since the regulations allowed a person to have two day's limit
in possession (6 fish) we decided it would make the hike more
worthwhile if we went late in the evening, caught one limit,
and then after midnight caught the rest and then headed for
home in time to sleep for a few hours before going to work.

An Angry Mother Bear

What we discovered when we arrived at this little fishing "paradise" was a little unnerving. As we approached the creek, we came upon a lone fisherman yelling and banging on his canoe as if his life depended on it. He told us that he'd floated down the river to this place and had been having good success when his peaceful evening was interrupted by a sow brown bear and her cubs who decided that he was in their fishing spot and started harassing him. His banging and hollering had temporarily frightened the bears off, but he was heading down the river and home to safety.

We were armed with our rifles and flashlights and decided that since, perhaps, the bears had fled the country, we'd just continue on as planned. So, we walked down the alder-lined banks of the creek a hundred feet or so to where the "fishin' hole" was and started casting away in the waning minutes of daylight. We hooked and lost a few salmon which did the usual salmon thing and started jumping and splashing around the pool trying to get free. This ruckus was all it took to signal the bears that supper was on the table, and they came crashing through the brush!

Hearing them coming started another commotion—our yelling!! That stopped them, but you could hear them just a few yards back in the alders snorting and growling a low guttural sound that caused the hair on the back of my neck to stand up! Then, it was silent. With a loaded and cocked rifle in one hand and a fishing rod in the other, we discovered that the joy of fishing was fast dissipating. The problem was that it was now almost completely dark and we weren't too anxious to start walking along that river bank with our backs to the bears. After another growling and snarling session by the bear trio, we decided that flight was our best option and we hightailed it for the tracks and, with the aid of our flashlights, did double-time hiking back to the car…fishless and weary.

Have you ever noticed how things that cause fear in your life always loom larger and scarier at night? On that river bank, as dark approached, every shadow and stump looked like a bear crouching ready to pounce!

Sasquatches … and Things That Go Bump in the Night!

That feeling of foreboding reminds me of another experience that occurred a few years ago while my wife and I were spending some time living at her family's remote cabin at 8000 feet in the Rockies above Steamboat Springs, Colorado. It was a dark, cold and stormy night in the fall and we had been reading the account of a friend of ours who was reporting that he had encountered a Sasquatch along the Pacific coast. Our friend is about six feet ten and was a former standout college basketball player before getting his doctorate in psychology and entering private practice. He was not and is not a nutcase, so we had read his account with interest. He said that the "big-foot" made him feel small and introduced him to a whole new realm of emotion ranging from fear to stark terror.

With visions of hairy monsters swimming around in our imaginations, we were more than a little edgy as things outside that wilderness cabin were banging and scratching as the wind and rain swirled around outside. The problem occurred when I needed to make a trip to town for some chilly night essentials (popcorn and cookies). Going out there into that pitch-black darkness was not my idea of fun but, being the "man of the house," it was my lot to venture forth. The car was parked about fifty feet away from the cabin so I sprinted at laser speed to get safely inside the car while my fearless wife bolted the door and made sure all the windows were latched. Any

Sasquatch visitors that night would have to go through a log door with a two by four bar securing it!! A half-hour later I arrived back home with the "goods" and made another Olympic class sprint through the dark to the door of the cabin and safety.

Now, my wife and I have been wandering the hills of Colorado, Alaska and Washington for most of our adult lives, and neither of us has come upon anything resembling a Sasquatch and, in fact, up until our friend's purported sighting, I figured that those who claimed to have seen one had their grits a little off the center of their plate or at least were prone to exaggeration. Bears we've seen plenty of, along with moose, elk, deer, lynx, wolverines, and even a few mink and marten . . . but no Sasquatch.

Analysis

So, what was happening that night on the river bank with the bears and that stormy night with the imaginary Sasquatches that would cause such jumpiness and apprehension? In retrospect, I believe it was the combination of *the foreboding darkness* outside and the *sense of vulnerability* that were all amplified by the mental images of huge creatures lurking about—out there!

The morning after our Sasquatch alert, as we sat out on the porch watching the stellar jays, chickadees and woodpeckers flitting around the bird feeders, we laughed at how silly we felt to have been so fearful. What was the difference? *The light!* Light drives away fear and gives us proper perspective.

Psalm 91 shares with us the incredible place of safety that is ours when we dwell "in the secret place of the most High [God]," and states that we don't have to be afraid of the terror that comes at night or anything that goes "bump in the dark"— *no matter how big his feet are!!*

CHAPTER 21

The Power of Positive Anticipation

E very year on Memorial Day weekend tens of thousands of Anchorage residents load up their cars, trucks, motor homes and campers and charge south en masse to the fishing grounds on the Kenai Peninsula. The tourists have yet to arrive in force, so this is an Alaskan phenomenon. It reminds me a little of the land rushes that I have seen depicted in movie westerns where the hopeful homesteaders all lined up on their horses and in covered wagons or buckboards, and at the sound of a gunshot they tore across the prairie at breakneck speed to be the first to get to the prime homestead sites. The difference, of course, is that on this Alaskan weekend, the "prize" is a good camping spot near one of the Kenai streams that host early runs of the much sought-after king salmon.

Alaska's Big Show

The craziness actually begins weeks earlier at the Great Alaska Sportsman's Show in Anchorage, attended by over a hundred thousand Alaskans where they can wander around for hours amongst the booths and displays of the latest versions of "must have" hunting, fishing, camping and hiking equipment. A good number of Alaska's guides, outfitters and lodges have booths there as well. And, there is the plastic swimming pool converted to a "trout pond" where wide-eyed little fisherpersons can dangle a hook and catch a fish. Outside there are rows of boats, RV's and four-wheelers for those who "lust" after the more pricey items.

I used to attend the "show" when the doors opened the first day and then I would try to make it back three days later just before it closed. I always thought it funny to see the change in demeanor among the vendors. Day one, they are all smiles and exuding high energy while eagerly fielding question after question. In the waning hours of the show, these same vendors are so weary of smiling and answering questions that some can be seen dozing off while sitting or leaning on their displays. The whole deal, though, is all about *creating excitement and eager anticipation* among winter weary Alaskans. The next few weeks seem like they just "drag" by at a snail's pace as these *wired* outdoors enthusiasts have to wait for nature to bring warmer days, thawed lakes and rivers, spring "break-up" and finally, the regulatory OK by the Fish and Game folks to "let the games begin!" By opening day, the coffee pot of anticipation is percolating at a full boil!

Gentlemen, Start Your Engines!

For several years, I used to park my car on the south edge of Anchorage and just watch as the frenzied drivers jockeyed for position and a quicker escape from the city. The look on their faces showed an intensity that said, "Get out of my way. I have this brand new motor home that cost me $100,000 and I am going to have fun this weekend…and if you get in my way,

I will run right over you!"

The comical sight at the other end of their journey is that hundreds of people had actually left town several days earlier and some campgrounds already display "Sorry, campground full" signs at their entrance. The rest of the story is played out a few days later when these road-warriors pile their sleep-deprived bodies back aboard for the long drive home. Have you ever noticed how hungry people entering a restaurant always walk faster than those leaving with full bellies? Same principle.

How Positive Anticipation Saved a Life

Calls from distraught people seldom come in the light of day! Usually they come in the dark hours of the night when fearful, depressed and sleepless folks get desperate enough to reach out for help. Such was the case one night during the Thanksgiving season when our phone rang around 1 a.m. and I found myself talking with a very suicidal lady who said she had a loaded and cocked handgun sitting beside her.

As we talked, she alternated between telling me glimpses of how she came to lose hope with living, amidst repeated threats to hang up and do the final act of her lonely life. In a nutshell, she felt rejected by everyone and she just couldn't face another holiday by herself. She was blind in one eye necessitating her wearing a patch. She was blinded when her enraged husband, while driving down the highway, had pulled a .45 from the glove compartment, shot her in the eye, and dumped her out of the vehicle, thinking she was dead. Miraculously, the bullet had entered her eye and traveled along the top of her skull before exiting out the back of her head without damaging enough brain tissue to kill her. After regaining consciousness, she actually walked to a nearby medical office where she got emergency treatment. For hours, I listened and tried everything I could think of to help this woman grasp a speck of hope on which to hang a reason to keep on living.

God's Intervention

Then, a thought came to me that I know was from God because, quite frankly, I was too tired and rummy to have thought of it. An individual had come into some extra money and had given me $300 as a Thanksgiving gift with which to buy some food for any needy families of which I might be aware. The lady on the phone didn't need money or food, but what I suggested was that she meet me later that day at a grocery store and we would together buy and distribute the food to some needy families. I was amazed when she accepted my invitation and sure enough, when I saw a middle-aged woman with an eyepatch approaching me in the Safeway parking lot, I knew it was her.

The transformation from the night before was incredible. The thought . . . just the *thought* that she could be involved in giving to someone else gave her a reason to live and a sense of value as a person. She was giddy and animated as she tore around the store picking out items that would "bless" someone on Thanksgiving Day. As we drove up to the house of the first needy family on my list, I handed her two bags full of food and said, "Here, you do it." By the end of our delivery route, she was in tears; only these were tears of joy! To my knowledge, that one ounce of positive anticipation and then actually *doing* something for others was a turning point in her life!

A Significant Life

In James 4:10 the Bible says that if we will humble ourselves before God, "He will lift you up and make your lives significant" (Amplified Bible). That is, He will make our lives *matter*. While humbling ourselves is hardly on our list of favorite things to do, if we take God at His promise, He will do His part and give us a significant life, one that is invested in the things that really count. Once we humble ourselves before God and add to it the power of positive anticipation (faith) that God will make our lives matter, even the seemingly arduous task of humbling, takes on a new sense of adventure. I don't know about you, but to me, having my life *matter* in the eternal Kingdom of God is about as good as it gets!

CHAPTER 22

Combat Fishing

The immense size of Alaska offers about one square mile of land for each of its residents. So you would think there would be plenty of room for everyone, including the million and a half tourists who drive, fly or cruise to Alaska every year in search of the adventure of a lifetime. The problem, however, is that only a small portion of the state is connected to a road system; those places easily accessible to everyone generally attract a crowd—and especially when it comes to fishing. While a short plane ride or boat trip to a remote area can put you in true wilderness isolation, it is sometimes a little costly or intimidating to charter a ride to the bush so most people stick to the closer places and create what is called *combat fishing* where the river bank can resemble a crowded subway station in the Bronx! If you want to see pictures of this, just go on-line and ask a search engine to help you find "Alaskan Combat Fishing." It seems incongruous that there can be that many people, standing that close together, flogging the water and actually enjoying it.

Russian River – the Combat Zone

The Russian River, about a 100-mile trip south of Anchorage, is a *combat fishing* stream when the sockeye salmon are running in June and July. Thousands of people jostle for the best spots hoping to catch a few of these feisty fish. If there is no place to fish, people often wait behind those fishing until someone in front gets a line tangle or a fish and wades to shore to take care of it. They just step right into the vacancy, and occasionally tempers flare when the replaced fisherman returns to reclaim *his* spot. It is also not unusual for someone to get hooked in the ear, nose or lip by an errant hook whizzing past them. The hospital in nearby Soldotna has a special paper human silhouette taped to the emergency room wall with the actual hooks attached that they removed that season from involuntarily pierced and smarting fishermen.

One sunny afternoon while joining in the "fun" with the other combatants, I had an "enlightening" experience that cured my itch for this type of fishing. Some people claim that the sockeye salmon's first run upon being hooked is so fast and furious that they consider it, pound for pound, the best fighting fish in Alaska.

Well, I came to agree with them when I inadvertently snagged a big, male sockeye near the tail and he tore across the river like a dragster in a hurry, peeling 50 or 60 yards of 20 lb. test line off my fly reel with impunity. Fearing that a fish I was going to have to release anyway was going to take all of my line and not look back, I clamped my hand down on the reel and felt the line tighten and stretch to the point where I knew it would snap. Instead, the hook tore loose and my hook, line, and sinker came right at me like a rifle shot! I could see that three-quarter ounce sinker headed right for my head and I thought, "Uh-oh—duck!"

But before I could move an inch, I heard an explosion in my head, saw flashes of light (enlightenment) and went down to one knee, semi-knocked out like I had just been clobbered by George Foreman, the boxer! The sinker had hit me on the forehead just above the bill of my baseball cap leaving a golf ball-sized welt and me one very woozy fisherman.

Unsurprisingly, not one fisherman even broke their casting rhythm to see if I was all right. I wobbled up the beach to catch the river ferry to cross back to the parking area where I took a nap, two extra strength Tylenol and made a vow that I'd rather fish in the bath tub than do that again.

Not long ago as I was preaching on the famous biblical story of David's battle with the nine-foot tall Goliath of the Philistines, I made an attempt to put myself in Goliath's shoes. Here he was, heavy-weight champion of the world in those days, with nothing but wins on his resume, when here comes this pip-squeak of a kid wearing his sheepherding armor (none) and carrying some sort of twinky sling-type weapon and a pocket full of rocks—the equivalent of hunting a grizzly with a BB gun! After he roared with laughter and was just cocking his massive spear-chucking arm to impale this little twerp, in a whir of motion he saw a sinker-sized rock heading right for the bridge of his Philistine nose. I can relate to just how he felt at that instant, and he may have thought, "Uh-oh—duck." But it was too late ... and you know the *rest* of the story. The size or type of weapon or enemy is irrelevant. When God is in your corner that's all that counts.

CHAPTER 23

"Your Most Endearing Quality"

Some of my most enjoyable assignments over the years have been traversing Alaska doing seminars and retreats for churches. Due to the size of the state (they say that if you cut Alaska in two, Texas would still only be the third largest state) travel often involved getting there by boat or plane which could sometimes be an adventure itself. But once you got there, it was usually a good experience . . . except this once when . . . .

Let Me Introduce You to . . .

I was leading the opening moments of a marriage seminar, and I had planned to have the participants introduce their spouses and share with the group (about 40 people) one of their spouse's most endearing qualities or what they loved the most about their husband or wife. The first ones I called on happened to be an older couple who were leaders in the church and whom I felt certain would introduce each other in a really loving way to get things started off right. I should have warned them they'd be first because the husband thought for a moment and said, "Well, this is my wife Ethel (not her real name), and her most endearing quality is . . . uh . . . well . . . er . . . . Aw shoot, I can't think of a thing!"

His wife, normally a really warm person, had thunder-clouds in her expression and daggers in her voice as she shot back, "You aren't so hot yourself either, buster!" as she headed for the door. Needless to say, that seminar got off to a very rocky start, and the next couples to introduce their spouses were quite profuse in saying kind things about one another.

A few years later, and hopefully a little wiser, I was leading a workshop in Anchorage for single adults and thought it was safe to ask the group at the beginning of the session to intro-duce *themselves* with what they felt was their most endearing quality. As these fine folks struggled to find one good thing to say, I realized that many people find it difficult to pinpoint and openly share anything good about themselves. Sharing faults or hang-ups seems to come much easier, but sharing qualities is hard. It isn't because they want to appear humble instead of prideful about their good points. Rather, it is too often the case that many people really don't think very highly of themselves and are much more in tune with their shortcomings than with their strengths.

In my many years of pastoral counseling, I have met pre-cious few people that I would consider truly "proud" individ-uals who believe that they are better than others. What I have seen are a lot of people who project a prideful appearing atti-tude or put down others as a cover-up for their own insecuri-ties and poor self-image.

Fish on . . . Fish Off

I have seen this dynamic played out many times while fishing for salmon in the icy, fish-filled waters of Alaska. It is not at all uncommon, while fishing on a boat with a group of other fishermen, for a person to hook a fish, but in the ensuing fight have the line break or the fish throw the hook. I'd say that most fishermen lose more fish than they actually land. What I have noticed is that when people who don't think very highly of themselves happen to lose a fish, or worse yet, don't even get a bite while others around them are hauling in fish left and right, they tend to take it personally and feel that they must be a flawed or cursed person because the fish got away.

I have seen people pout, cry, throw tantrums, snap fishing poles or throw them into the water and make those around them wish they'd stayed home! Those who are OK with themselves as people, though disappointed at losing a fish, will generally just exclaim, "Yehaw, that was fun," put on more bait and go after another fish!

This reveals a truth about human nature that is worth mentioning here. That is, most of us have a tendency to simply be too hard on ourselves. While the Bible does teach us to examine ourselves and to put off our "old nature" with its sinful ways and seek the Lord's help in building good and noble character qualities, it also says that it is completely acceptable to acknowledge every good thing that is in us (Philemon 6).

True humility is not a cringing, self depreciation or sense of shame about who you are. It is an honest and sober evaluation of one's self that, in reality, does include some pretty good stuff that the Lord has developed in each of us. The Biblical injunction to love our neighbor as we love ourselves begins first with learning to love ourselves.

"I Do Toast!"

Now, I am not saying that we should go around extolling our virtues to anyone who will listen, but I am saying that it is a healthy thing to give God, yourself and others some credit. Once while leading a divorce recovery workshop, I had let the group up for a breather in the midst of some pretty intense material by asking them to share with others if they had a particularly good recipe they would be willing to pass on to anyone interested. After a half-dozen or so of the ladies shared that they did good lasagna, various soups, and an omelet or two, one handsome guy in the front row finally worked up the courage to raise his hand and share his claim to culinary fame by saying, "I do toast!" You've gotta start somewhere!

CHAPTER 24

Once in a Blue Moon

I remember reading a book once comprised of stories about church life that was written by a clergyman at the end of his career in which he was recounting tales that he could not tell while he was still pastoring churches. Not wanting to embarrass anyone, he tactfully shared some of the humorous or downright bizarre things he'd observed about people in some of their less than shining moments.

It reminded me of the joke I heard once about a pastor who was always getting in hot water by telling uncomplimentary ethnic jokes from the pulpit. Finally, the church board took him to task about this habit and encouraged him with instructions that if he were going to tell an ethnic joke, to pick some extinct tribe or people group so no one present would get offended. The next service, he figured he had the solution and picked the Hittites of the Old Testament who had been obliterated. Having never met a Hittite, he felt safe in launching into a joke by saying, "You see, there were these two Hittites walking down the road one day, one named Sven and d' other named Lars . . . " Oops.

Well, here are a couple of Alaskan Hittite stories that occurred while I was pastoring a church in a galaxy far away—where truth is sometimes stranger than fiction.

Sagging Britches

He was quite a well-known evangelist with a good track record for encouraging congregations with his unique style of ministry, so we invited him to speak at our church for a three-meeting series. However, when I met him as he got off the plane, I hardly recognized him because he had gotten braces, permed his hair, lost a great deal of weight, and only barely resembled his public relations photo. After confirming he was indeed our guest, I showed him to his room next to the church and gave him some instructions on how to get around the city with its winter coating of ice and snow. Being from a much warmer climate, he was shivering at just the thought of going out in the frigid weather. He made a point to tell me that he'd brought along a pair of thermal long-johns and was going to wear them, even to church.

Well, he was about midway through his Sunday morning message when it became apparent to everyone sitting on the platform that indeed he was wearing his beloved long-johns. What had happened is that, months before coming to our church, with new braces on his teeth and a serious weight loss program, he had managed to take off over fifty pounds. However, he had not replaced his suits yet with clothing that would fit the new version of his body. Being somewhat absent-minded and not used to an extra layer of clothing, when he put his belt on his trousers that morning, he had inadvertently only gotten it through the front two loops. The back of the belt was unattached to his pants.

As he was moving around behind the pulpit, his already baggy britches came loose in the back and began sagging further and further down his long-john clad derriere! The extra layer of thermal material prevented him from feeling any cool breezes that might alert him to his dilemma. Every time he would wave an arm, the cut in the back of his suit coat would spread apart and everyone to the north of him got an eye-full. What do you do in a case like that? Walk up behind this well-known person in mid-sermon, and jerk his pants up or interrupt him with the news that he was mooning the choir?

My big mistake was that I happened to glance back at our choir (about 50 members that day) and saw two of its most faithful and godly soprano members laughing so hard that they had tears running down their faces. They would try to compose themselves only to have our oblivious speaker make another gesture that revealed an even fuller moon causing them to lose it again. It was all I could do not to burst out in laughter myself as the sermon drew to a close. By this time, he was actually standing on at least six inches of his pant cuffs that had worked their way down below and under the heels of his shoes.

As was his style, he started to walk down the three steps to the right of the pulpit, to floor level where he would pray for and minister to folks, but when he hit the second step, he finally realized that there was a problem, and in a move so smooth you hardly caught it, he hitched up his britches and didn't miss a beat. After he was finished, he sat down next to me on the platform, leaned over and whispered to me, "Hey man, I think I almost lost my pants up there, did you see that?" In my most somber and sincere voice, I evaded his question (as a good hearing aid wearer can) with another question, "See what?" I didn't have the heart to tell him he'd been mooning the choir for most of his sermon.

Personally, I don't think those two ladies in the choir were the only ones with tears of laughter running down their cheeks. That one probably had the Lord and a few squadrons of angels cracking up as well.

Foxhole Promises

Foxhole promises are those vows we make when we get in a fix and call out to the Lord for help, including the addendum that if He will come to our rescue, we will reciprocate by being better people or by changing some behaviors that are less than godly! The problem, of course, is that our memories usually get foggy and our promises are forgotten when our problem is fixed and our comfort zone restored.

One day, however, at the end of a church service as I stood below the platform talking with some people, a large, rugged looking man dressed in muddy coveralls and boots came walking down the center aisle with a sense of purpose that was a little unnerving. He strode right up to me and asked gruffly, "You the preacher?" When I replied that I was he said, "Come with me." Not knowing him from sic'um, I was a little reluctant to follow, but he was persistent and up the aisle and out the back door we went.

When we reached the parking area, he opened the back of his pickup canopy, reached in and grabbed a dead goose by the neck and handed it to me saying, "Here! My boat was about to sink in heavy seas coming back from huntin' these geese and I promised the good Lord that if I got back safe, I'd give a goose to some preacher. Well, you're it and here you are! Enjoy it." He promptly hopped in his truck and drove away, leaving me standing there in the parking lot in my three-piece suit with a stranglehold on a grease and grit-covered dead Canadian honker and chuckling to myself, "...Only in Alaska!"

ZZZzzz ...

Occasionally, people who haven't learned acceptable church protocol may do or say things that tax your ability to maintain a straight face, like the time a man fell asleep on one end of my counseling couch while his wife was on the other end delivering a thirty minute monologue on what a lousy husband he was. He awakened when his elbow slipped off the arm rest, and I asked him, "Well, what do you think about that?" Not having a clue of what I was talking about, he responded sheepishly, "I'm just here to save my marriage!" She didn't laugh! I tried not to.

Or, there was the time during a late afternoon counseling session, while listening to a story by a client with an especially soothing voice, I nodded off to sleep myself. I had been up most of the night before with a sick parishioner and my client could see that glazed look in my eyes. He laughingly asked if it might not be better if he came back another day!

Dear Mr. Jesus

One day our church accountant knocked on my door with a dilemma. It seems that someone had put a check in the offering box that was made out to JESUS. It was a counter check with no printed name or phone number on it and the signature was illegible. She wanted to know what to do with the check. We both began to laugh when we considered that maybe I could take it to the bank and see if they would cash it. The problem was that I didn't have the nerve to endorse it as Jesus. Forging a check to him might be hazardous. And, we could just imagine the bank teller saying, "Ah yes, so *you* are Jesus! We had the apostle Paul in here just yesterday!" We eventually took the check to the bank and discovered the donor's name through his account number.

That last story reminded me of a church member named John who had been on a job assignment to communist China. While it was forbidden for him to openly talk about Christianity or Jesus, he had managed to clandestinely distribute some booklets with some quotations from the Gospel of John. He had printed his stateside address on them in case somehow one of them found its way into the hands of a genuine seeker after God. He was overjoyed when he returned to the USA and found a letter waiting for him. The letter was short and sweet and it went something like this, "Dear Mr. Jesus. I have read your book and liked it very much. Please send me more pages if you can." While he had the personnel confused, I would not be surprised to meet him in heaven someday when there will be no doubt about *the real Jesus!*

CHAPTER 25

Baptizing "Stephan Fraser"

Wearing a hearing aid has been a bittersweet experience. While it is such a treat now to be able to hear the murmuring of a mountain brook, the song of a robin, or the scolding of a squirrel, there are still limitations that are frustrating . . . like when a battery goes out in the middle of a sermon, or while trying to hear someone with a soft voice that even the best of hearing devices can't pick up.

The Discovery

My discovery that I had a hearing loss happened in an unusual way—while baptizing people. Back in the mid-eighties I was involved in starting a new church in Anchorage, and we were using a school building for our Sunday services and a borrowed church for our midweek meeting. The church we were using had a baptismal tank, so any baptizing we needed to do we did there.

It was a frigid February night when it became my turn to do the baptizing and there were a half-dozen or so new converts eager to take this step in their spiritual journey. We had called the pastor of the church to make sure he turned on the heater in the tank so it would be warm enough to be comfortable. The baptismal tank was located along the north wall of the church auditorium and the second my foot hit the water, I knew, without a doubt, that the pastor had forgotten our request for warm water. It was hovering just above freezing!!

Knowing that the *show must go on*, I waded down into the deep end trying not to gasp when I got waist-deep. I do think, however, that my voice must have gone up an octave or so because that water was bitter cold! To spare my baptism subjects the shock I had experienced, I didn't linger long with pastoral comments and prayers, but immersed them as quickly as I could.

My big mistake, however, came after the last person came shivering out of what felt like the Bering Sea and I asked if anybody else wanted to be baptized. To my surprise, a young boy, about 10 years old, raised his hand saying he did. I had known all the other participants because I had taught a brief class to them the week before on the significance of water baptism, but I didn't recognize this young lad. Not wanting to embarrass him, I did a "Price Is Right" imitation and invited him to " . . . *come on down.*"

Once in the water he was too short to see over the edge of the tank, so I held him suspended partially in the water and asked his name. While I was mostly numb from the cold, he was shaking like an aspen leaf in the wind and between his chattering teeth I thought I heard him say, "Stephan Fraser."

"Well, Stephan," I asked, "have you accepted Jesus Christ as your personal Savior and do you understand why you are doing this?" I heard a few snickers in the audience when I said I was going to pray for *Stephan* and then baptize him. The laughter was unusual at such a moment, but I prayed anyway and was about to dunk this little believer under when the laughter became more widespread. Pausing, I asked in a puzzled voice, "What's so funny?"

His mom, sitting in the front row (she was also new and I hadn't met her either) said for all to hear, "His name isn't Stephan Fraser!" A little confused, I turned the boy toward me and asked him, "Son, I thought you said your name was Stephan Fraser . . . what *is* your name?" He replied through his shivers, "My name is *Mike*, and what I said was . . . 'this stuff is freezin'!'" The audience exploded into laughter!

I invite you to say those two things: "Stuff is freezin' and Stephan Fraser." You may see how a hearing-impaired person might make a faulty interpretation of the name. Well, I joined in the laughter at myself, baptized Mike, and now had about two hundred witnesses attesting to the fact that maybe I needed to see an audiologist. Not wanting to admit I had a chink in my masculine armor, it took me a few years before I finally made an appointment and learned that indeed I did have about a 40% loss in my left ear and slightly less in the right. At last I understood why I could never hear those modern new travel alarms that just chirp or peep.

All who worked with me were relieved at not having to repeat their questions or comments to me when I finally got hearing aids. I was in my mid-forties and was amazed at how many women approached me asking if I would please talk with their husbands and encourage them to stop being so proud and get their hearing tested.

"Cut 'er loose!"

One November election evening in Anchorage, I was sitting at a table at "Election Central," the Hotel Captain Cook, talking with an old Alaskan pioneer about his life experiences and discovered that he had a hearing loss as well.

As the election results began trickling in, precinct by precinct, we began talking about our experiences with hearing loss and hearing aids. He told me about his discovery of needing help with his hearing while flying in a small airplane with a load of gear lashed to the floats to be dropped from the air at the site of a remote camp. He was in the back seat and his job was to yank a rope at the pilot's signal which would release their cargo at low altitude and reduced speed so that it would drop unharmed at the target area, thus saving the hunters a ton of work packing the stuff the hard way.

Evidently, the drone of the airplane engine lulled him to sleep en route and he was in that dreamy state when the pilot spotted a huge moose below and began to circle it, just check-ing it out. This change in flight motion awakened and disori-ented him and he groggily asked the pilot, "What's happening?"

"There's a moose!" the pilot yelled over the noisy engine. What he heard in the back seat was, "Cut 'er loose!" and thinking it was time to drop their payload, he yanked the cord—miles from their intended campsite and from a much higher altitude than planned. Watching helplessly as their gear splattered all over the tundra below, he sheepishly concurred with the pilot that perhaps he might need to get his hearing checked. We both enjoyed a hearty laugh that only a couple of fellow hearing loss sufferers can fully share.

Gratitude

Personally, I am extremely thankful for that "moment" of discovery of my own hearing loss because my quality of life has been greatly enhanced by being able to understand when Marveen says *she loves me* and I don't have to reply, "Huh?" I will always be grateful to Joyce Sexton, one of Alaska's most patient and skilled audiologists who would not give up until I had hearing aids in my ears that work for me. Her sense of humor helped me over that initial characteristic "Alaska male" hesitation at admitting I was indeed *not invincible*! I am also thankful to my wife for her patience and for her having a job which provided health and auditory benefits so that I could afford to get the hearing aids I needed. We shared tears of joy the day I got my first hearing aid and we stood next to a waterfall—and I could actually hear its music.

Sometimes I Squeaketh!

Now, only occasionally do I have embarrassing hearing-related moments. A couple of years ago, while my hearing aid was being repaired, my audiologist gave me one of those "behind-the-ear" models to use as a loaner. They use a different technology than the "in-the-ear" type that I wear, and I soon discovered that the spongy temporary part that fits in the ear canal would occasionally work its way out causing a squealing sound that for some reason I could not hear.

While wearing this loaner, I had a counseling appointment with a mother and her adolescent son. About midway through the session, the little boy politely interrupted me while I was sharing a bit of advice with them by timidly saying, "*Sir, uh, your ear is squeaking!*" We had a good laugh as I replaced the earpiece and I was reminded of that verse that I can't seem to locate in the Bible that says, "Thou shalt not take thyself too seriously!" I also have to smile when I remember when my sweet, but ancient, Aunt Hattie Bryson, who had a profound hearing loss and a constantly squealing hearing aid, would ask the usher taking the offering in our little church in a "whisper" that everyone could hear, "*You got change for a twenty?*"

CHAPTER 26

One of my favorite places in Alaska is Turnagain Arm, a body of water connected to Cook Inlet that extends about forty miles south of Anchorage. It was named by the explorer Captain James Cook, who had to turn his ship around and hightail it out of there when he encountered the huge tide variations and treacherous sand bars. The tides here are the second highest in the world, and when they come roaring in they often create a wall of water several feet high called a Bore Tide.

The glacial silt and mud on the bottom can also be deadly if a person gets caught in it when the tide comes rushing in. The mud looks solid at first, but if you stand in it for a few minutes, it begins to get soupy. And if you sink in it, it is very difficult to pull yourself out. Since I moved to Alaska many years ago, there have been numerous fatalities as unwise or unsuspecting people underestimate the danger and don't live to tell about it. I heard one story where a helicopter rescue was attempted and when the chopper tried to pull a stuck person out with a rope attached to them, the person was so stuck in the mud they actually were pulled in two. It gives me goose bumps to think of what that must have been like for the victim, the family, and the rescuers.

Turnagain Tides

During the coldest part of winter, huge ice floes and icebergs move up and down this shoreline, grinding and groaning as the tides carry them along. At low tide, the whole Arm can be almost empty of water except for a few channels that look like raging rapids. Occasionally, brave (or a little wacky) windsurfers venture out on windy days wearing wetsuits to ride the waves and winds that can move up and down the Arm up to 100 mph. In the fall, huge schools of alabaster-white Beluga whales cruise in and out on the tides feeding on the late arriving silver salmon that run up the Arm to clear-water spawning streams. I actually have a fantasy of what it would be like to put a herring on the end of my fishing line and toss it out into the silty water with the possibility of actually being able to say that I once had a whale on my line! If it weren't illegal, I'd probably give it a try.

Fishing a High Tide

A hundred miles further south from Turnagain Arm is Seward, resting at the head of Resurrection Bay. Tides here are much milder but a high tide can be exciting here for different reasons. I carry my tide table booklet in my pocket all summer long and when the tides are just right, fishing along the shore in Seward can be incredible! Numerous times I have caught a limit of two kings or six silver salmon in a half hour or so on a rising tide. That's good fishing!

High Tide at Abbott Loop

No, Abbott Loop isn't a body of water with fish in it. It is a street in Anchorage with a church on it called Abbott Loop Community Church where I was blessed to serve as a pastor from 1974 to 1980. Founded in 1959 in an old Quonset hut on the fringes of south Anchorage by former banker Dick Benjamin, his family, and a few faithful friends, this church literally exploded as the Jesus Movement and the oil boom hit Alaska in the early 70s. Looking back, I think all involved would say that this was simply a sovereign move of God to have such a bountiful harvest of souls. It was like the tide came in and the nets were brimming with fish. It was not unusual during those years to have fifty or sixty people accept Christ every month! The church was in a constant building program for years! Part of the church vision was the planting of new churches by sending out teams of people to new cities and, in just a few years, around a hundred baby churches were established. New folks were coming in faster than we could send them out.

As a pastor, I felt like I had grabbed a moving train that literally jerked me off my feet. There were numerous pastors on the staff of the church and another thirty or so dedicated elders, and we had a challenging job trying to provide pastoral care for such a rapidly growing flock. We eventually began having home meetings, overseen by elders, to provide small group interaction for people. Some of those were larger than most of the churches I had pastored in the past.

On one occasion I delivered a sermon on the sometimes less than inspiring topic of tithing (giving). At the end (and to everyone's surprise), when I asked if there were any folks there who wanted to accept Christ, *seven* people immediately came forward to make that commitment! Another time, after a few rousing songs by the choir to open the meeting, Jim Brenn, one of the pastors with an incredible gift of bringing people to the Lord, went to the microphone, gave a simple invitation, and *sixteen* people walked the aisle to accept Jesus as their savior—all before the opening prayer! For several years, we just kept the water warm in the baptismal tank all the time. It felt like we were experiencing what Jesus had in mind when he told Peter that if he'd follow Him, He'd make him a fisher of men. This was like fishing at high tide at the peak of the salmon run!

I am sure that I could fill many pages with stories about those days at ALCC. Some would be of glorious victories, and I imagine I could also dredge up memories of some of our most inglorious and agonizing mistakes, of which there were more than a few. But I will just say that it was a blessing of a lifetime to be a part of what God was doing during that special time of harvest.

Probably one of the most memorable moments during those years happened one Sunday evening when, at the close of the service, one of the more spiritually sensitive members came to a microphone and delivered what she felt the Lord had wanted her to say. She said, "There is someone here tonight (there were about a thousand folks present), who sat on the edge of your bed earlier this evening and drank two bottles of beer in order to work up the courage to be here. Jesus wants you to know that He loves you and He is waiting with open arms for you right now." Immediately, a young man seated near the back shot his hand up in the air and loud enough for everyone to hear, yelled "Ya got me!" as he literally ran to the altar and to Jesus.

A story is told about how John Muir, famous naturalist and writer, once climbed a tall tree along the Northern California coast, and strapped himself to it so that he could discover what it felt like to experience the full fury of an incoming storm. He was a brave man. It was not enough for him to just read of the accounts of others; he wanted to see for himself. Like most things in life, the real excitement is in the doing, rather than being a spectator. (*The Life and Adventures of John Muir,* James Mitchell Clark, Sierra Club Books, 1980).

If I read my Bible correctly, in these final days before the return of Jesus, the action in His kingdom is going to get pretty exciting. Just like those brave surfers who catch the churning wave of an incoming bore tide on Turnagain Arm, I pray that we will be ready to move with God should that *Kingdom Bore Tide* happen in your area or mine. In the meantime, ". . . let us not be weary in well doing: for in due season we shall reap, if we faint not" (Galatians 6:9, KJV).

CHAPTER 27

Mr. Marveen
Goes to Juneau

Juneau, the capital city of Alaska, is undoubtedly one of the most unique seats of government of any state in the Union. You can't get there from here! Well, at least by road you can't. Juneau, located on the Lynn Canal in southeast Alaska, is accessible only by boat or airplane. There have been dreams of connecting it to the highway system, but the cost and thought of marring that beautiful coastline with a roadway seems too big a price to pay. So, people keep taking the ferry or, when the airport isn't fogged in, they fly into the capital. When the sun shines, Juneau is unrivaled in its beauty and magnificent scenery. The ocean there is so clear that you can look down into thirty feet of water and watch starfish and crabs creeping along the bottom.

A Special Moment

Juneau is a special city to me for reasons other than its scenery, governmental activities, and gold rush history. It is the place where my wife, Marveen, was working when I asked her to marry me in the spring of 1991. After about two years of pondering, praying and enjoying each other's company, I looked into my heart and decided it was time to see if she were willing to take that serious step. At the time, she was working as the chief of staff for an Anchorage senator and was in Juneau for the five-month legislative session. So, I flew from Anchorage to Juneau, rehearsing in my mind just how to present my proposal.

Marveen met me at the airport and we drove in her old '72 Blazer out along the ocean, past the ferry terminal at Auke Bay to the Shrine of Saint Therese, a beautiful retreat center with a gravel walkway out into the sea where an alcove of trees surrounds the chapel. It was a foggy and chilly day with rain squalls blowing down the canal. On the ocean side of the chapel was an overlook providing a panoramic view of the water and surrounding islands. We had the whole place to ourselves except for a huge humpback whale that was cavorting around about 200-yards offshore.

After a few minutes of conversation, we just stood there in silence, soaking up the ambiance of the moment, even though the rain was starting to make us shiver with cold. I think Marveen sensed that I had something I wanted to say so she just let me dangle there in silence for a few minutes while I was searching frantically for all those introductory lines I had planned for this moment.

But my mind was blank except for a silent prayer that I had been sending heavenward. It went something like this: "Lord, if asking Marveen to marry me is OK with you, would you please make that whale out there in the water "breech" (jump clear out of the water) for me." There were lots of factors to consider when marrying in mid-life and neither of us wanted to make a mistake. So both of us had been seeking God's direction in earnest.

Well, five, ten, fifteen minutes went by and that pesky whale just kept spouting and fiddling around in the water while we were both starting to get really cold. Then, suddenly, ol' Moby Dick surfaced and slapped the water with one of his huge front flippers! That was good enough for me so through chattering teeth, I *boldly* stated, "You know, Marveen, you would sure make a good wife!" She smiled and allowed that I might make a good husband as well as we headed for the car and some warmth.

As we passed by the entrance of the little chapel, I thought, "That was a pathetic proposal if I ever heard one. You can do better than that, Wayne." So, I took her in my arms . . . right there in front of Saint Therese, looked her in the eyes and asked her, "Marveen, will you please marry me?"

"Yes, I will" was her reply as we hugged, kissed, breathed a mutual sigh of relief and hightailed it to the Blazer. About fifty yards down the highway, the reality of what we had just done and all the changes that it would bring, began to settle in our minds as we drove silently back toward town. We agreed to "wear" this decision for a month before we would tell anyone.

A Shotgun-less Wedding

Later that year we got married on a rocky overlook high in the hills above Anchorage. We had planned to get married at a special spot along Turnagain Arm, but on the day of our wedding a huge brown bear and her two cubs were napping in the exact spot we had in mind. The Park rangers had closed off the area so we moved the location to avoid having, literally, a *"shotgun"* (for protection) wedding!!

After a year hiatus from the Legislature, including a stint working for the Division of Elections in Anchorage, Marveen was offered a chief of staff position with another legislator and the Juneau/Anchorage rotation began again for her. I was counseling and doing seminars in Anchorage and her job took her to Juneau from January to May for the session. While her intense position didn't allow for many (if any) trips to Anchorage during the session, my schedule was flexible, so every three or four weeks I'd fly down to spend a week or so with her in her little apartment a block from the Capitol Building where she worked.

Marveen's World

Being in Juneau around the daily functioning of state government was fascinating to me. This was Marveen's world and I quickly discovered that she was a highly respected person with a reputation for putting in tireless effort and long hours to make sure that legislation her boss was proposing or considering was studied from all angles. Her natural thoroughness and perspicacity made her a valuable employee. I was (and still am) very proud of her and what she accomplished there.

During my visits, I would often sit in the visitors' gallery and listen to the debate on whatever issues were on the floor. However, it didn't take long before the word got out that I was a pastor and soon I was asked to serve as a daily chaplain when I was in town with the assignment of offering the invocations at the beginning of the day. Sometimes I would pray for the House session at ten and the Senate session at eleven.

I really enjoyed the challenge of writing and offering meaningful prayers to God in a setting like this where editorializing or preaching through your prayers to a captive audience is frowned upon. But the more I got acquainted with the legislators and their families, the easier it became to pray honestly and with compassion. I always breathed a sigh of relief when the House Speaker or Senate President would entertain a motion that the prayer be entered into the daily journal and the legislators always voted "Yea" instead of "Nay." I guess that was their way of saying, "Amen!"

I was really blessed the day that Representative Gail Phillips, who was then the Speaker of the House, told me that she was blessed by one of my prayers to such an extent that she had it framed and mounted on the wall of her office in the Capitol Building. Being a lawmaker and decision maker is not always what it appears during a campaign or on the evening news. It is a very difficult job and I applaud these servants of the people of Alaska for their hard work and dedication.

In 1996, I happened to be doing the opening prayer for the House of Representatives the day a photographer took a panoramic picture for their annual group portrait. I was honored to be asked to stand in with them right next to the United States flag. When the 12"x36" pictures were distributed, Marveen had all of the representatives sign a copy for me which now hangs framed with pride on my office wall.

"Take a Breath, Wayne"

As I mentioned earlier, this was Marveen's world. The church in Alaska was my home turf so to speak, so when I visited Marveen, it was a whole new arena for me. I actually worked for three days one time as a pinch-hitter receptionist in Marveen's office when she worked for Representative Cynthia Toohey, a respected, feisty, and straight shooting legislator from Anchorage. What an experience!

My job was to answer the phone a few hundred times a day, take messages, make appointments for Representative Toohey, and try not to mess things up and embarrass my wife. I remember my first early morning call when I stammered out,

"Representative Toohey's office, may I help you." I must have sounded pretty tense because I heard the Representative in the other room laughingly call out, "Take a breath, Wayne, it will be all right!" After just three days of working in the trenches of Juneau life, I gained a huge respect for what my wife did everyday for thirteen years. I now understood why some days she would come home from the office and just need to sit quietly or take a quick nap before engaging in conversation or dinner.

Meet Mr. Marveen

I have a vivid memory of an encounter in a Juneau restaurant with another legislative staffer with a position similar to Marveen's. I had met her once before so on this occasion she attempted to introduce me to the person with whom she was sharing lunch. She launched into the introduction but suddenly had that panicked look on her face as she completely forgot my name. After a second or two of awkward silence, she blurted out, "Oh, shoot, I can't remember his name. He's . . . he's *Mr. Marveen!*" We had a good laugh about my new title as I made my way to my own table where I began to mentally process this.

Now, I am pretty secure in my manhood, so I had no issue with that. I have been referred to as Wayne, Pastor Wayne, even The Reverend Coggins on occasion; but never Mr. Marveen. However, as I thought about it, I had to smile and allow that considering Marveen's hard-earned and well-deserved good reputation in Juneau and among her peers, I'd just wear my new name with head held high. I am blessed, happy and proud to be Marveen's husband and would answer to "Mr. Marveen" anytime.

The Coveted Lujon

The Anchor River was high and muddy from spring run-off that day, so king salmon fishing was slow for my two fishing buddies and me. Ed Crutchfield, Don Shields and I had logged many fishing trips together since we had all arrived in Alaska near the same time in the early 70s. We had attended the same church during college days in the Seattle area and the three of us had all succumbed to the lure of Alaska. Many hours together driving to and from fishing adventures had forged a close bond between us that is often rare among men in our society.

I always admired Ed and Don, partly because they were so gifted at doing things that I couldn't do worth a hoot! The other part was that they were honest guys who loved their families and tried with all their hearts to serve and follow the Lord's direction in their lives. They were great allies to have in the battles of life.

The Big Silver Lure

After hours of unsuccessful fishing, I felt a tug on my line and I set the hook in what I hoped was a big king salmon. I held the line tight, expecting that first powerful run by a fish not happy with a hook in his mouth. Instead, my line was immobile and I had that sinking feeling that I was about to break off yet another hook on a snag or rock that I hadn't been able to detect in the murky water. I tried the usual tricks to dislodge the hook and finally took a couple of wraps of line around my forearm and stepped back a few feet expecting the line to snap with a loud report. To my surprise, I felt something give way and I reeled in what I imagined was a branch or clump of roots from the bottom.

When I got it to the shore, I discovered that my hook had managed to snag a huge fishing lure called a Lujon that had been lodged on the river bottom. A Lujon is a heavy silver jig-type lure that is used in Alaska to catch halibut in deep waters offshore. This one had a few feet of about 80-pound test line attached, and it didn't take a brilliant deduction to figure that someone had been using this big lure with its over-sized treble hook to illegally snag salmon (almost a felony in Alaska).

A Tradition Is Born

As it turned out, that catch was the only one any of us made that day and it was a long five-hour drive back to Anchorage with no fish to fry! I think it was on the drive home that one of us came up with the idea to engrave "The Coveted Lujon Award" on the silvery side of that big lure. And the next time we went fishing, the one who caught the biggest fish would get to keep The Coveted Lujon until the next trip when it would go up for grabs again. It was the source of many laughs, and over the years it spent most of the time in Don's tackle box . . . an indicator of who among us was the best fisherman.

As often is the case in our world, after a few years our paths began to diverge and those "Three Stooges" fishing trips just became part of the repertoire of tales we told our kids and grandkids. Ed and I (along with about fifty others) headed to the east coast to plant a church, while Don and his family stayed on in Alaska where he taught school and took frequent mission trips to Peru and Russia with his family. Ed eventually settled in Oregon, and I returned to Alaska, and while we would occasionally talk about a rendezvous to compete for that Coveted Lujon, it never happened and Don is still the keeper of the prize.

Ed Crutchfield

Then, about two years ago, we got word that Ed, who had always been a good athlete and had kept himself in excellent shape, had been diagnosed with a rare and rapidly growing cancer in the lining around his intestines. While Ed, his family and all of us who loved him, held on to the end with hope that God would spare his life, he went home to be with the Lord. A few months before that happened, I was able to fly down to Oregon and spend the better part of a day with Ed.

It just didn't seem possible that Ed was dying, but a look at his battle-weary smile told me that this was a bigger battle than any fish had ever given him. We sat in his living room talking about old times, dumb things we had done and the things that really mattered in life to him as he was seeing the end of life's runway coming up fast. Then, we went to a park where all of his children and their families gathered in the shade of some huge rhododendron trees and a professional photographer took pictures of everyone with Ed. When it came time for me to leave, we hugged and prayed together and the last time I saw him was through teary eyes in my rear view mirror as he leaned on his wonderful wife, Linda, and waved goodbye.

The other day, Don and his family visited the church where I am pastor in North Kenai. It warmed my heart to see my old friend again, and we had a good talk about his new adventures and mine. Eventually, we got around to talking about Ed, fishing, and The Coveted Lujon. We concluded that maybe we should put that thing up for grabs one more time and go fishing again. Then, a brief but awkward moment of silence lapsed between us as I think we both realized that it just wouldn't be the same without Ed.

I think I will talk to Don the next time we're together and see if he would be willing to just keep that Lujon close by, and if Jesus returns before we die, grab it and take it up where the River of Life flows and see if we can round up Ed and the three of us scout around to see if there are any salmon there.

CHAPTER 29

Old Groaner

There is a fascinating Alaskan story about a legendary grizzly bear known as "Old Groaner." The gist of the tale is that, back in the mid-1930s, two prospectors searching for gold in the wilderness kept hearing an eerie, mournful moaning and groaning in the woods around their camp at night. It sounded like someone or something in a lot of pain out there in the foreboding darkness of the forest. It was unnerving, and over the course of several years this bear harassed them, yet he always managed to stay out of sight.

In the end, the mystery was solved when the enormous, almost completely hairless grizzly charged one of the miners who shot and killed it at close range. A close inspection revealed that "Old Groaner," as they had nicknamed him, had numerous broken teeth, a jawbone that had been crushed but never healed, five bullets lodged in his skull and only scar tissue where one eye had been. It was a wonder that the bear was still alive. The sorrowful groaning was the sound of unrelenting pain that "Old Groaner" lived with every day (*The Alaska*

Book, J. G. Ferguson Publishing, 1960).

Bear Hunting on Purpose

Only once in my life have I ever gone brown/grizzly bear hunting *on purpose*. Any time you are salmon or trout fishing on remote streams in Alaska you are in bear country, and it is wise to be armed in case an unpredictable bear decides to become aggressive protecting a fishing spot or moose carcass it has stashed nearby. The time that I did go bear hunting on purpose turned out to be quite an adventure. Three friends and I decided that we'd try a spring brown bear hunt in the Iniskin Bay area on the west side of Cook Inlet in the foothills of the Alaska Range. Early spring, when the bears first come out of hibernation, is one of the best times to take a bear if you can find one before he rubs out his thick winter coat leaving bald or thin spots.

My hunting partners included Bob Chapman, a resident of Anchor Point and son of Sherm and Vi Chapman who homesteaded what is now the little community of Anchor Point on the Kenai Peninsula. The other two were Jim Brenn, an Anchorage area pastor, and Marshall Ellison, then an Anchorage credit union manager and very gifted pianist. I figured that I'd be in good company with these savvy woodsmen as we tackled one of Alaska's most challenging hunting adventures.

We chartered a ride in a DeHaviland Beaver float plane with veteran bush pilot Bill DeCreft and loaded our gear and a week's supply of food aboard this workhorse aircraft and headed west from Homer across the Inlet to our Iniskin Bay destination. There was still a lot of snow on the mountains and along the shores of the bay but we found a relatively grassy spot near a small creek where we set up our tent on the nearest thing to level ground.

As it turned out, the day we flew in there was about the only decent weather day we would have for the duration of the hunt. In fact, the first night there it rained so hard that the little creek beside our camp overflowed its banks and a branch of it came running right through our tent and into Bob's goose down sleeping bag. Sometime around three or four in the morning I awakened to sounds outside the tent and discovered Bob trying his best to get a fire going with soggy wood so he could get dry and warm. When I got up to help him, I could see that he was suffering from a degree of hypothermia because his hands were shaking so badly that he couldn't even strike a match. Eventually, with the aid of some of our gas we got a roaring fire going. Dawn of the first day of our hunt finally came.

Arctic Refrigerator

One of our discoveries at our camp spot was several large icebergs that had been left high and dry at the high tide line. One, about the size of a refrigerator, had numerous hollow spots in it where we could conveniently store the dozens of eggs that we'd brought along. What we hadn't counted on was that downpour of rain that melted the ice, causing it to collapse and crush our breakfast egg supply. I have a photo someplace of Jim, the designated egg scrambler, wringing out a cardboard carton of eggs over a big skillet. I remember well that crunching sensation as we all discovered that more than a few broken eggshells escaped into the "mulligan" omelet we devoured that first morning.

Avalanche Country

In spite of a driving, bone-chilling rain, we pumped up our

Avion inflatable boat and motored out into the bay in search of a beach-feeding bear. About mid-morning we started hearing avalanches break loose from the high peaks as the rain-laden snow began to get too heavy to hold in place. It sounded like a thunderstorm as the snow and ice would crack and then rumble down the canyons to the beach below. It was quite a show.

Later that first day a commercial fishing boat came into the bay at high tide and dropped off another hunting party of three Army men who took their gear ashore in their low-sided skiff. The following morning we saw them waving for help as we went out to look for bears again and found that they had not moved their boat far enough inland and the night's high tide had carried it away leaving them stranded. We kept a lookout for the boat that day but I think it probably got carried out to sea and likely sank in the waves. Their first day of hunting didn't go much better than ours.

Finally, a Bear!

On about the fifth day of hunting in the rain, we rolled out of our sleeping bags and decided to raid our cache of food and fix the biscuits...the kind that come in a tube. They can be pretty tasty when "baked" on an open grill with Jim's favorite Nabob strawberry jam. The problem was that the bottoms tended to burn while the middles were more than a little doughy, but being hungry we each devoured about ten biscuits and then sat around the campfire moaning about the glob of dough that seemed to be rising in our extended bellies. Suddenly, one of the guys spotted movement on one of the slopes behind our camp. It was a huge male brown bear traversing his way along a snowy ridge. We grabbed our rifles and all four of us took off to see if we could intercept this big trophy and get a shot at him.

Trying to climb up a mountain in several feet of soggy, wet snow without snowshoes turned out to be an exercise in futility as we were sinking up to our thighs with each step. Finally, about a thousand feet up the slope we hit firmer snow and picked up the bear's trail. When we neared the top of the ridge, we assumed that the terrain on the other side of the slope would be traversable. However, as we peeked over the edge, what we found was that we were standing on a wind-formed cornice of snow and ice and literally were standing in mid-air with no solid ground under our feet. In unison we backed slowly away from the ridgeline to plan our next move. Not wanting to trigger an avalanche and have to surf the thing to the bottom far below, we opted to let the bear wander the high country on his own and we'd head back down to sea level.

When we finally reached our camp, we dragged our weary bodies on Jell-O-like legs to a log and sat there for quite awhile being numbly grateful not to be under a mountain of avalanche snow and ice. It was about then when the effects of all that exertion and adrenaline showed up and the fermenting yeast in our bellies from all those half-baked biscuits had all of us looking a little green around the gills. I think we skipped lunch, but we were happy because at least we had *seen* a bear.

After several days more of monsoon winds and heavy rain, our scheduled rendezvous with our pilot came and went. When he did finally arrive, he told us that the weather was so bad that he'd only be able to take two of us out in order to carry the extra fuel that he might need to get home. Jim and Marshall, needing to get back to Anchorage to their jobs, went out on that first trip leaving Bob and me with a dwindling food supply and no sure time when the pilot thought he could make it back. We took stock of our remaining food and figured we'd need to forage for some clams to augment our instant oatmeal menu.

At the next low tide we harvested a bucket full of big white clams that were plentiful around the bay. While I have gone to fancy seafood restaurants and gobbled down a dozen or so of those delicious little butter clams, these guys were in another league when it came to chewing time. They were indeed a change of pace from oatmeal!

A few days earlier we had spotted an abandoned hunting camp in a little cove off the bay, so Bob and I decided we'd check it out while waiting for our plane to arrive. What we discovered gave us the chills. It was obvious that the camp had been abandoned in a hurry and hadn't been visited since the previous fall. There were no human tracks in the snow. Sitting on the table in the nice wall tent with a wooden floor and a little stove was an opened box of cereal, a bowl, and a spoon. Behind the tent, partially covered in snow were several decomposing bear hides.

Late that night with the wind still howling and rain coming down sideways buffeting our tent, Bob and I began thinking and talking about the "Old Groaner" story and wondered if perhaps the boss hunter or caretaker had been getting ready for breakfast when he heard a groan outside and having gone to check it out, became breakfast himself for a big bear. I think it was about that time when Bob, normally a pretty reserved guy, asked me if I was having fun yet?! We both laughed a nervous laugh but slept lightly that night.

About mid-morning the next day we heard the most welcome sound of a small plane circling and getting into position to land and take us back to warm beds, dry clothes, good food and HOME. As we were lifting off from Iniskin Bay, I looked down on our barren campsite, and the end of Psalm 30:5 came to me about how "weeping endures for a night but joy comes in the morning." That sure was the case and this was my last "on purpose" bear hunt! This was enough of an adventure and survival test to last me for a lifetime.

Over the years, we have relived that abysmal hunting trip and observed the old principle that after the misery or danger of the experience has abated, the things a person tends to remember are the humorous or heroic moments that occurred. These days, however, the only "Old Groaner" grizzly I hope to meet is the one who lives in the Alaska Zoo in Anchorage. May he live long and prosper!

CHAPTER 30

Things Grow Fast Under the Midnight Sun

Much of what is written about Alaska has to do with the extremes of ice, snow, and those long hours of winter darkness. But if you ask any Alaskan what possesses them to actually live in such a frozen land, their eyes will sparkle when they say, "Ah, let me tell you about the summers and the midnight sun!"

A Land Of Extremes

Yes, it is true that there are several months of the year in the far north when the sun doesn't set at all, and in the south-central region it only dips down for a nap for a few minutes each night. In Anchorage, it is not unusual to hear lawn mowers fired up at midnight, and a common sight is aluminum foil covering the inside of window panes to hopefully block out the light so those inside can get some sleep. The July 4th fireworks display is often somewhat less than exciting because it is too light to see the colors. It is also not uncommon for many Alaskans to start coming down with colds or other ailments around mid-summer because their bodies are so run down from lack of sleep.

Giant Cabbages

All of that bright sunlight makes for a very short, but prolific growing season. The Matanuska Valley, about fifty miles northeast of Anchorage, with its rich soil and warm sunny days *and* nights is famous for growing huge vegetables. It is not unusual to find cabbages that weigh in the neighborhood of a hundred pounds!

Every year, just before Labor Day, these monster cabbages and other super-sized vegetables are loaded up and hauled to the Alaska State Fairgrounds in Palmer to compete for braggin' rights for another year. Nearly half the population of the state will attend this big celebration to mark the end of another summer of frenzied activity and spit in the eye of another winter, knowing that in a few short weeks the frost will hit, the leaves will drop, and the geese will get in formation and head south! An old friend in Seward used to gleefully welcome the days when the cold weather would drive the "weenie roasters" (tourists) away and she could walk on her favorite stretch of beach all by herself.

Arctic Churches

While the "growing season" in Alaska is a flurry of activity, I have noticed that not everything in Alaska grows as fast as those cabbages! Sometimes growth comes slowly for churches in the far north. Oh, there are some that experience meteoric growth from time to time, but as a general rule, it is slow going. I occasionally read of urban churches in the "lower 48" that grow from zero to thousands in just a few short years. That might be a tough act to follow here in Alaska where the total population of the town may only be 150. It takes a special kind of person with steel for a backbone to labor in some of these remote and often lonely outposts. I am certain that registration day in heaven, when these gospel pioneers sign in, will reveal to everyone their worth from God's point of view.

Swamp Spruce

Swamp Spruce, also known as Bog Spruce or Black Spruce, is an amazing testimony to slow growing, tenacious living in less than favorable conditions. Thriving in bogs and swamps as their name implies, these little giants of the forest seem to survive where little else can grow. I have returned to old fishing or hunting areas to find the same trees looking exactly like they did ten or twenty years before. They are weather and temperature hardened as you will discover if you attempt to saw one for firewood. It may have taken these unheralded swamp dwellers decades to reach shoulder height.

I think I have met more than a few people who fit into that same category. They are tough as leather and hardened by adversity but still full of the life flow of God's Spirit, which keeps them standing when others have given up. They are the anchors of their communities, families and churches . . . often working behind the scenes to lighten the load of those in need.

Though Swamp Spruce trees may dwell in the shadow of their taller and nobler looking cousins, the Sitka Spruce (Alaska State Tree), if I am in need of some tough timbers for a tough job, I just might look first in the swamp. I think God does.

CHAPTER 31

Fisher of Men

During the summer months the Talkeetna River is a fast-moving torrent of gray, silt-laden, glacier water with numerous sweepers and logs lying just below the surface to gouge a raft, ding a propeller, or worse. It is not a safe place for novice jet boat owners to learn the limitations of their craft, nor is it a place to even consider taking an under-powered or low-sided boat. Just about every year, my friend, Steve Mahay, is called upon to rescue stranded boaters, attempt to salvage their sunken boats, or look for bodies. The numerous sharp corners and log jams on this river have become the graveyard for more than one unwary outdoors-man. For that reason, Steve maintains a fleet of high-sided, very powerful and finely-tuned aluminum jet boats to ferry fishermen, hunters and sightseers to this incredibly beautiful and bountiful area.

Steve and his crew of boat drivers are safety conscious to the extreme and are most often the rescuers of others. When you board their boats and are seated with your life jacket securely on, they do a head count and call "Mahay Base" on their CB radio with the message of how many "souls are aboard." I think that is a nautical expression, but it does serve to remind you that anything can happen and you had better have your soul in good connection with God.

Miracle on the Talkeetna

One day in late summer, after a season of rain and high water, we decided to hop a ride with Steve up to Clear Creek for some silver salmon fishing. While waiting at his loading area I struck up a conversation with two gentlemen who were waiting as well. I learned that Steve had just recently rescued them from a treacherous log jam up the river and, after dropping off us fishermen, was going to help them try to salvage some of their gear.

They said that the engine on their low-sided, flat-bottomed boat had stalled and they were swept by the swift current into a log jam, overturning the boat. One of the guys had managed to jump free of the boat to the log jam. His partner, though, was sucked under the water and trapped under the logs, in almost certain danger of drowning. Frantic to help his friend, though he could see nothing in the turbid, churning water, he jammed his arm as far as he could below the surface and *miraculously* his hand wrapped around the wrist of his drowning buddy. In a motion driven by super-human strength, he literally jerked his water-soaked friend out of the water and up onto the logs beside him; a feat he admitted that he could not have done with his own strength.

Talking with me, they were still both visibly shaken by their experience and acknowledged that God indeed had intervened, and they gave Him credit for being able to tell the story and go home to hug their families. I imagine they gained new perspective on the importance of that outstretched hand that Simon Peter experienced.

Miracles on the Sea of Galilee

Simon Peter, a savvy and successful fisherman on the Sea of Galilee, had been cleaning his nets with his brother Andrew, when Jesus turned his life upside down by inviting him to, "Follow me, and I will make you fishers of men" (Matthew 4:18-19, KJV). Both men immediately left their nets to see what this carpenter from Nazareth could possibly mean by such an invitation. They had met Jesus, the Messiah, and after following Him and learning about His kingdom, they saw many miracles including the feeding of five thousand people with a few fish and pieces of bread (Matthew 14:15-21).

It was immediately after this miracle that Peter and the other disciples encountered heavy seas and were indeed fearful of capsizing. Suddenly, Jesus appeared to them, walking on the water, causing some to think it was a ghost. Peter, however, recognized Jesus, and when He invited Peter to walk to Him on the water, he hopped out of the boat and began to miraculously walk on the water himself. However, when fear of the waves caused him to doubt, he began to sink. Keep in mind, he hadn't read the end of the story yet. Calling out for Jesus to save him, Jesus did just that and reached out his hand and "fished" the fisherman out of the water, saving his life.

I believe it is a valid point here that for Peter to become the "fisher of men" that Jesus had predicted he would become, he needed to be rescued or saved himself, by the Master. Shortly after this event and after Jesus' betrayal by Judas, His death on the cross and resurrection, Peter found himself fishing again. And after a night of fishless toil, he saw this same Jesus on the shore. Jesus urged this veteran fisherman that if he'd just cast his net to the other side of the boat, he'd find fish. Realizing that he'd never been given bum advice by Jesus before, he obeyed and bingo—their nets were full to the point of breaking.

A few weeks after Jesus departed Planet Earth, Peter, fresh from some serious repenting for denying being a follower of this Man from Galilee, and energized by the Holy Spirit, stood and addressed a huge crowd of people. And after his first sermon, *casting the net for men*, three thousand people accepted Christ. A few days later, another five thousand responded to this fisherman's call to become Jesus' followers.

Centuries later, even an old Alaskan like me has to admit, *that* was pretty good fishing. And, the good news is that Jesus is still inviting us to follow Him and enjoy fishing where the prize is not just a few fish to eat or sell, but for the eternal souls of men and women. In fact, if you have never accepted Christ as your savior, you are much like Peter, going under and needing Jesus' hand to rescue you. Call out to Him. He will stretch His hand out, grasp yours, and never let you go.

• • • • •

For information on other books, seminars and counseling offered by the author, visit his website at:

www.CornerstoneFamilyMinistries.com.